Becoming a Woman

Becoming a Woman

Simone de Beauvoir and the Politics of Trans Existence

Megan Burke

polity

Copyright © Megan Burke, 2025
The Author hereby asserts their moral right to be identified as author of the Work.

First published by Polity Press in 2025

Polity Press
65 Bridge Street
Cambridge CB2 1UR, UK

Polity Press
111 River Street
Hoboken, NJ 07030, USA

All rights reserved. Except for the quotation of short passages for the purpose of criticism and review, no part of this publication may be reproduced, stored in a retrieval system, or transmitted, in any form or by any means, electronic, mechanical, photocopying, recording, or otherwise, without the prior permission of the publisher.

ISBN-13: 978-1-5095-6198-8 – hardback
ISBN-13: 978-1-5095-6199-5 – paperback

A catalogue record for this book is available from the British Library.

Library of Congress Control Number: 2024936775

Typeset in 11 on 13 pt Sabon by
Cheshire Typesetting Ltd, Cuddington, Cheshire
Printed and bound in Great Britain by CPI Group (UK) Ltd, Croydon

The publisher has used its best endeavors to ensure that the URLs for external websites referred to in this book are correct and active at the time of going to press. However, the publisher has no responsibility for the websites and can make no guarantee that a site will remain live or that the content is or will remain appropriate.

Every effort has been made to trace all copyright holders, but if any have been overlooked the publisher will be pleased to include any necessary credits in any subsequent reprint or edition.

For further information on Polity, visit our website:
politybooks.com

Contents

Acknowledgments vi
Preface vii

Introduction: Trans Antagonisms and Beauvoir 1

1 Becoming a Woman 26

2 On Females and Women 51

3 An Ethics of Trans Affirmation 74

Conclusion: Bad Faith and Feminism 104

Glossary 114
References 120

Acknowledgments

To all the trans and queer accomplices, past, present, and future, creating space for expansive possibilities – thank you. To all those in the places with whom I've found myself and didn't expect to find myself, thank you for showing me that it's possible to build worlds and make new meaning together. I would never have understood with such richness that being-with is what it takes. For those whose ideas have inspired me, especially to the trans philosophers who I've had the privilege to think alongside and learn from; to Gonzalo and Maia, for reading this early on, and carefully and with enthusiasm; to a few loves, who took interest in my ideas and cared for me in various ways while I was writing this book; to my mom, always. To Elise for being supportive of the project, full stop; for trans people everywhere living and doing the best they can in this world, thank you.

Preface

While writing this book, it has often felt like anti-trans forces are becoming mundane. They are not, of course. Their persistence is concerning. The social and material power wielded by those who espouse anti-trans views and those who create and advocate for anti-trans legislation is alarming. They are creating, and maintaining, a world where trans and gender-nonconforming people are targets of violence and have diminished life chances. Because today's anti-trans sentiments frame trans people, and trans women in particular, as well as gender-nonconformity, as predatory and pedophilic and as a risk to the freedom of girls and women, they are sentiments being adopted by those who don't know very much about trans existence in the first place.

This is a book about this contemporary social and political climate, and about what's wrong with it. It is also about how some self-proclaimed feminists weaponize a classic feminist text to justify transphobia. That text is Simone de Beauvoir's *The Second Sex* ([1949a, 1949b] 2010). Often dubbed the feminist bible, *The Second Sex* offers an indictment of patriarchal ideology as it shapes and violates women's lives. It has, for years now, been drawn on by gender-critical feminists

Preface

as a means of trans exclusion. Although a niche in the world of trans antagonisms, this manifestation of anti-trans politics is disturbing. This anti-trans mobilization of Beauvoir aims to offer a reasoned justification for denying trans experience. If the views of one of the most famous feminist philosophers of all time show that trans experience is dubious, that real women are *never* trans, then anti-trans sentiments are not political after all; they are just the truth, even if the truth hurts trans people. As a Beauvoir scholar, I've been disturbed by the anti-trans turn to Beauvoir. I continue to be disturbed the more it persists. If it's not yet disturbing to you, my hope is that this book will show you how it is and why you ought to be concerned.

In this book, I offer an alternative reading of Beauvoir that challenges gender-critical turns to her work. Given that Beauvoir herself was not focused on trans experience – which does not, I think, mean her work is not relevant to it – my reading also shows how Beauvoir's commitments and her analysis in *The Second Sex* speak to and support trans existence. Through this reading, I hope readers learn about *The Second Sex* and what Beauvoir is really up to in the book. I also hope to offer a window into the general social and political landscape of trans antagonisms in Western contexts, especially – but not only – for people who don't know much about what's going on.

In this book, I use **transgender**, or **trans** for short, in a descriptive way, not as an identity category. I follow, though loosely, Susan Stryker's notion of the term in *Transgender History*, in which she uses transgender/trans "to refer to people who move away from the gender they were assigned at birth ... *the movement across a socially imposed boundary away from an unchosen starting place* – rather than any particular destination or mode of transition" (2008, p. 1). This is not the only way to define transgender/trans, and it is not necessarily an agreed-upon definition amongst trans scholars or trans people more generally. I use it here because I take it to be a helpful heuristic for describing the broad range of experience targeted by anti-trans politics and sentiments. At the same time, how an individual is targeted and the extent to which they are impacted has everything to do with the entirety of their social positioning, including their race, class, sexuality, and national origin. It is certainly the case that trans people of color, and trans women of color, have long been the most vulnerable of trans people, the most deeply impacted by hostilities toward trans people.

I write this book as a white, middle-class, queer, non-binary American academic. As many people do, I have a complex relationship to gender. As I will talk about at several places in the book, some of my experience feels like a trans experience, though of a very privileged kind. Some of my experience does not. I don't care to reconcile this ambiguity here, for myself or for you, the reader. I may never care to reconcile this ambiguity; it is one way I have come to assume my existence. As I hope this book makes clear, despite what some people may claim, there are many ways to live out who we are as sexed and gendered people. There should be many. In writing this book, my intention is not to speak for all trans people or all variations of trans experience. My intention isn't even to speak about the many, many creative ways trans people inhabit the world and seek to change it. Rather, I've tried to draw attention to what and who is getting in the way of trans existence. More importantly, I've tried to make clear that trans possibilities are valid and why everyone ought to create conditions for their flourishing.

Introduction: Trans Antagonisms and Beauvoir

On March 11, 2024, right around the time I was completing the final edits on this book, an article by trans scholar Andrea Long Chu was published in *New York Magazine*. The article, "Freedom of Sex: The Moral Case for Letting Trans Kids Change Their Bodies," offers an important trans account of freedom. The account is, on the one hand, an intervention in the hostile landscape of anti-trans politics and, on the other, an intervention in leftist politics that argue for trans affirmation on the basis of gender alone. Chu not only argues that trans kids should not be denied transition-related medical care, but also, and most importantly, she argues that securing the freedom to choose one's gender *and* one's sex is the morally right thing to do. Chu puts it this way: "What does this freedom look like in practice? Let anyone change their sex. Let anyone change their gender. Let anyone change their sex *again*" (2024). Chu insists on defending the desire of trans kids who wish to change their biological sex, regardless of where the desire comes from. For Chu, as the freedom to pursue gender in different ways has changed, "the number of people wishing to change their sex" has increased. "Sex itself," she writes, "is becoming a site of freedom" (2024, p. i).

Becoming a Woman

In a world rife with anti-trans politics, Chu's position is as powerful as it is provocative. It challenges us to conceive of what is possible – to at least confront, if not entirely reimagine, how we could pursue our embodied lives and how we could allow others to pursue theirs. Her conception of freedom relies on challenging commonly held assumptions and beliefs about the meaning of sex and gender. Or, as she puts it, "In general, we must rid ourselves of the idea that any necessary relationship exists between sex and gender; this prepares us to claim that the freedom to bring sex and gender into whatever relation one chooses is a basic human right" (2024). This book is written in this spirit.

Put most succinctly, the positive ethical position at the heart of this book is that trans people's self-determined existence should be affirmed, which is to say, honored and supported. Such affirmation is a condition necessary to securing trans life chances. To disavow trans people's self-determination and eliminate the material conditions in which trans people can realize who they are is to create genocidal social and political conditions for trans people. This may sound like an extreme claim, but granting authorial social and political power to efforts and views that disavow trans people is a way to produce trans *non-existence*. This book highlights legislative actions and gender-critical perspectives as two extreme and powerful forms of such disavowal, but it is also baked into many social conventions and traditions in more nuanced ways, in ways that often don't register as hostile or transphobic. At the same time, the ethical position of this book is not just about securing trans life chances; it is about working for and securing a world of care and justice, a world that resists austerity and domination.

Securing this ethical position and pursuing freedom that affirms trans lives does require intervening in beliefs

Introduction: Trans Antagonisms and Beauvoir

and perspectives that erode and erase trans possibilities. What is also required is a reconsideration of how we should understand sex and gender. Often, mainstream discourse around trans affirmation or trans exclusion is captivated by the discourse of gender identity and is thus captured by a concern with *the nature of sex and gender*. This concern with metaphysics is not the only way to consider the meaning of sex and gender. This book insists we need to shift our attention. By turning to the philosophical work of Simone de Beauvoir, this book prioritizes an ethical not metaphysical ground for trans affirmation. Rather than get trapped in the issue of *what* trans people are, or *what* sex and gender are, Beauvoir's work demands a prioritization of *how* we all choose to live together.

The Turn to Beauvoir

It's a curious turn. Simone de Beauvoir, author of *The Second Sex*, published in 1949 and often dubbed the feminist bible, is certainly not at the forefront of contemporary politics over trans existence. If non-academics have heard of Beauvoir, they likely haven't studied *The Second Sex*. Beauvoir also didn't write about trans people. Beauvoir was concerned with the situation of non-trans women in a world dominated by men. Today, Beauvoir's work is, at times, mobilized to denounce trans existence by predominantly white, non-trans women from Western countries such as the United Kingdom and the United States who call themselves **gender-critical feminists**. Gender-critical turns to Beauvoir can be found within academia, as well as without. As will be discussed in more detail soon, what these turns to Beauvoir share in common is a claim that Beauvoir emphasizes that to be a woman is a matter of sex, not gender. One of the more notable references to Beauvoir can be found in the well-known and controversial blog post made by the author of the Harry Potter series on June 10, 2020. It is often the case that gender-critical discourse turns to Beauvoir to insist that *real* women are born women, which delegitimizes trans existence. In *Gender-Critical Feminism*, philosopher Holly Lawford-Smith sums up who such feminists are: "These rebels call themselves gender-critical feminists, referring to the idea that gender is something we should be critical of" (2022, p. xii).

For some time, being critical of rigid gender norms and their imposition in individuals' lives has been a central feminist practice. Gender-critical feminists, however, make their target the reality of gender identity. Rather than seeing the imposition of rigid gender norms as a key site of patriarchal oppression, gender-critical feminists take the insistence on gender identity to obfuscate the oppression of women *as females*. Their concern is to not only fight for the liberation of non-trans women, but also to situate the site of their oppression in the reality of sex. They take a focus on gender, which they claim to be the focus of trans activists, to be the political erasure of sex. Gender-critical feminists rebel and fight in the name of sex, against the new tyranny of gender. In doing so, they inspire suspicion of trans people and, as a result, of affirming trans existence. Instead of affirming trans people, full stop, the gender-critical view insists we should be asking: Is it *really*, as trans activists claim, trans people who are oppressed? What if trans activists are deceiving all of us, especially the youth, into thinking that being trans is not only real, but also a reality that should be supported? In all the contemporary fervor about trans rights and trans affirmation, what is happening to "real" women?

Philosopher Kathleen Stock's book *Material Girls: Why Reality Matters for Feminism* (2021) exemplifies

Introduction: Trans Antagonisms and Beauvoir

a gender-critical turn to Beauvoir. According to Stock, Beauvoir's account of what it means to be a woman is incorrectly leveraged by trans affirmative politics, or what Stock refers to more pejoratively as "gender ideology," which she takes to be a tyrannical set of misguided beliefs about the reality of gender as an identity that one chooses for oneself. For Stock, the most famous sentence in *The Second Sex* – "One is not born, but rather becomes, a woman" – is one of the key moments in the formation of gender ideology, but not because Beauvoir herself meant it to be (Beauvoir, 1949b, p. 13). For Stock, this sentence has been interpreted to mean that a woman is not born, but is socially constructed, which means that a woman is not a woman by birth but is something one becomes. From this interpretation, it follows that a transgender woman is a woman without qualification because she has, as Beauvoir claims, *become* a woman. But for Stock, as she says in an interview, "I don't think she [Beauvoir] had any conception of how that phrase would be used, but it set in motion a chain of thought and processes. That sentence is used all the time to justify the idea that trans women are *literally* women, or even that gender identity makes one a woman" (Gluck, 2021).

In her own effort to denounce gender identity and challenge the view that trans women are women – that is, real women in the metaphysical sense – Stock claims that Beauvoir's interest was not in gender, but in sex. The name of the book was *The Second Sex*, after all. What gender-critical discourse does is claim that it is sex not gender that is the marker of reality, that makes one a *real* woman. Whatever this thing called gender is, they claim, whatever gender identity one might claim to have is, in effect, *not real*. This move toward sex is at once political and philosophical. The claim is not only that contemporary trans activism obscures the reality of *sex-*

5

based oppression, or the oppression of women, but that affirming trans existence also mystifies what is real: sex is real, gender identity is not. Although gender-critical feminists, such as Stock, who do turn to Beauvoir are not scholars of her work, the author of the feminist bible nonetheless occupies an interesting place in the gender-critical push to shift our focus to sex – and not merely away from gender, but *against* it.

There is so much to say. But let's stay with Beauvoir for now; doing so will clarify her relevance to thinking about and affirming trans existence. Beauvoir's famous sentence does inaugurate an important distinction for feminism, but it's not the one Stock claims. Stock's misreading is not entirely her fault. Decades of academic feminists, particularly those in the Anglo-American context, have misread Beauvoir's famous sentence. In the sentence – "One is not born, but rather becomes, a woman" – there is a classic philosophical distinction between being and becoming. This distinction is a metaphysical one about the nature or essence of reality.

Being refers to an internal, predetermined, and unchanging essence of a thing, whereas **becoming** refers to the reality of a thing as indeterminate, historically bound, and therefore contingent. Because Beauvoir was an existentialist through and through, across all her work, she rejects the idea that there is any such thing as a predetermined human nature. Who and what we are, Beauvoir believes, is a result of human agency in the past and present. This belief is central to *The Second Sex*. When she claims that one is not born, but becomes, a woman, her point is that women are not by *nature* women, which means that, on her account, there is no such thing, naturally, as a **natal woman**. In fact, her most famous sentence targets the view that takes women to be women by virtue of biological facts, by virtue of what Stock and Lawford-

Introduction: Trans Antagonisms and Beauvoir

Smith refer to as biological sex. Beauvoir believes it faulty to accept the commonsense idea that to be born with certain genitalia or reproductive capacities *makes one* a woman. In Beauvoir's language, becoming a woman is a **social destiny** imposed on, and taken up or lived out by, a certain group of human beings. As will be further discussed in chapter 1, far from a biological fact, Beauvoir's account of becoming a woman as a social destiny shows how the conferral of 'woman' onto an individual by others is an enforced structure of lived experience. Furthermore, even if her account focuses on the imposition of this social destiny onto specific sexed bodies, such a social destiny is a product of human actions and choices. Ultimately, her account shows how non-trans existence is naturalized and normalized, which makes being a woman an immutable, natural fact. This is not the view Beauvoir endorses but one she exposes and argues against. In contrast, the gender-critical thrust insists on the realness, and thus truth, of biological sex.

In Beauvoir's view, **biological essentialism**, or the belief that physiology or biology is the essence of a woman, is erroneous. "[H]umanity ... is a historical becoming," she asserts in the conclusion of *The Second Sex* (2010, p. 753). We are not what and who we are because of our biology. 'Woman' is not found in any essence called 'sex.' And yet that still leaves us with the question of how to understand and articulate the relation between physiological differences and the reality of 'woman' – or, that is, as Beauvoir makes clear, that women clearly do exist in the world in *a certain way*, in relation to being female. But, as this book shows, Beauvoir doesn't understand this relation between being female and a woman to be a necessary or essential relation. That is, it's not a law of nature. It is not an inevitable reality. This does not rule out the significance of physiology; indeed, it shows how sexed embodiment is an experiential dimension of our existence, not a determinative and fixed one.

For Beauvoir, we *become* who we are, and this includes the very existence of women as female, a point that urges us to reconsider not only the relation between 'woman' and 'female' but also what 'sex' and 'female' even are. This reconsideration is a needed response to the gender-critical reliance on the naturalness of sex. Whether and how 'female' *and* 'woman' are lived and experienced is a collective endeavor; we have the power to limit or open our possibilities. Working from Beauvoir's most famous sentence, then, this book highlights how Beauvoir's feminist philosophical and political commitments are trans inclusive and why we should heed her insights today.

Trans-Exclusionary Feminism

For those not versed in the history of feminism, the concerns of gender-critical feminists may seem new. They may even sound legitimate. They may even resonate. But they are neither new nor uncomplicated. They are, rather, central to a long line of allegedly feminist texts in the Anglo-American context that advance arguments to discredit transgender existence. Since at least the 1970s, there has been a select group of non-trans women, often but not exclusively lesbian women, who rally under the banner of feminism and denounce the reality of trans existence. Janice Raymond's 1979 *The Transsexual Empire* is an inaugural text in this lineage – Raymond herself says she "probably was designated as the first Terf." In her work, Raymond insists not only that trans women are men, but also that the very existence of trans women is another way patriarchy rapes "real" women (Bindel, 2021).

Introduction: Trans Antagonisms and Beauvoir

TERF is an acronym that stands for "**trans-exclusionary radical feminist.**" TERF was created and popularized in 2008 by feminist blogger Viv Smythe, a non-trans woman. Then, and now, TERF names people, usually non-trans women, who claim to be feminists, that support the freedom of women and stand against the injustice of patriarchal domination, but also espouse views or offer support for views that, in various ways, delegitimize the existence of transgender people. Feminists who are called TERFs generally denounce the label TERF, claiming it to be a slur that aims to silence them, akin to misogynist epithets like "bitch" and "whore," slurs women are accustomed to fielding in a male supremacist world that seeks to censor their perspectives. Views of TERF as a slur suggest that the people who deploy it conspire against the freedom of non-transgender women.

Raymond's argument *is* exclusionary. It denies that trans women are women outright. It also obscures the reality of violence insofar as trans women are more likely to be victims of rape than perpetrators of it. In more recent years, Sheila Jeffrey's 2014 *Gender Hurts* argues that trans existence harms non-trans women, and considers trans men to be victims of patriarchal trauma who, if healed, would be women after all. Trans manhood is thus read as a maladaptive response, rather than as a legitimate way of being in the world. Abigail Shrier's popular 2020 book, *Irreversible Damage*, pushes the maladaptive narrative even further, insisting that trans boyhoods must be prevented because they are first and foremost a mode of defective social adjustment that adolescents adopt by being influenced and groomed by trans adults. Drawing on the pseudo-scientific hypothesis of Rapid Onset Gender Dysphoria (ROGD), which posits that trans identities that emerge during puberty not only do not last, but also are the product of a social contagion in which adolescent "girls" are duped into thinking they are trans, Shrier's ultimate aim is to encourage the prevention of trans boyhoods, an aim that gets off the ground by disavowing who trans boys say they are by insisting on the truth of biological sex. Giving voice to a widely held commitment in gender-critical discourse, Shrier insists it is best for girls to remain girls who become women, even though such a view goes against trans people's self-knowledge and the recommendations of organizations like the American Psychiatric Association and the American Medical Association. Although, as will be discussed in chapter 3, these organizations have not always been supportive of trans existence, and reliance on medical authorities to legitimize trans existence is full of problems, gender-critical perspectives dismiss outright the established credibility of these medical recommendations.

At the heart of this feminist history, in its past and present formations, is a philosophical debate over the meaning of what it is *to be* a woman. The gender-critical view claim is that being born a woman means one is a woman by virtue of one's biological sex, making one what gender-critical views often call a **natal woman**, or a woman by virtue of biology. This biological fact, it is claimed, makes a woman a *real* woman. On such a view of 'woman,' there is a distinction made between natal women and trans women. Trans women are neither natal women nor real women, but cosplaying 'woman' by virtue of claiming to have an innate gender identity. The gender-critical view insists not only that natal women are the only real women, but that trans activism is out of hand – indeed, duping all of us. Rallying around gender identity, gender-critical activists insist, is not going to make any of us free; it's just going to harm "real" women. Rallying around trans activism is not

Introduction: Trans Antagonisms and Beauvoir

going to end oppression; it's just going to harm "real" women. Affirming the lives of trans people by way of affirming their gender identity is not going to make anyone free; it's just going to harm "real" women.

Throughout the book, I use the term "gender-critical" not to minimize the clear trans-exclusionary commitments those who hold gender-critical views have. I take gender-critical feminism to be today's version of trans-exclusionary feminism. I have chosen to take up that language of gender-critical because it is in the world as such. My hope is to expose what it stands for, to make clear that it is trans exclusionary no matter what we call it.

At a time when the lives of transgender youth and adults across the world are still largely precarious, vulnerable to numerous forms of discrimination and violence, and in which there is an onslaught of genocidal legislative efforts targeting trans people in various nations, the questions and concerns raised by gender-critical views are worthy of scrutiny. What sense should we make of the surge and presence of gender-critical ideology in today's social and political landscapes, ones that, across the world, are increasingly antagonistic and hostile toward the possibility of transgender life? Are their concerns legitimate? And if they are not, as this book suggests, on what grounds can and should we affirm trans existence? What does it mean to affirm trans existence? In response to contemporary trans antagonisms that include, but are not restricted to, those generated by gender-critical perspectives, this book works from these questions by turning to Beauvoir. In making this turn, this book unpacks Beauvoir's conception of 'woman,' highlighting how it is trans inclusive, and, in doing so, shows why we ought to, and how we ought to, affirm trans existence.

Becoming a Woman

The Reality of Trans Antagonisms

There has been a substantial increase in anti-trans legislation and public opinion in recent years in the United States. This legislative escalation has been apparent in the US since at least 2015. It was a response to what *Time Magazine*, in its May 2014 issue featuring Laverne Cox, dubbed the "transgender tipping point" to describe the increased visibility of trans people in pop culture, and a response to the 2015 Supreme Court ruling in favor of marriage equality and the Obama Administration's moves to offer protections for gender identity under Title IX provisions. The politics of the Trump Administration not only fueled the anti-trans legislative fire, but also incited more latent anti-trans hostilities to enter the public sphere. In the US, by the first four months of 2023, there were over 400 bills introduced across state legislatures targeting the life chances of trans people, doubling the number of legislative attacks posed in all of 2022. As of July 2023, there are 18 states that have passed bills that make it impossible or extremely difficult for trans people to amend identity documents with their actual name and gender, to safely access public bathrooms and other gender-segregated public facilities, to participate in public sports, and to access healthcare. Public education, from elementary schools to higher education, and public entertainment, especially in the form of drag performances, have also been under attack, with various bills banning content that speaks about sexuality and gender in ways affirmative of lesbian, gay, bisexual, and transgender people. Under a heavy-handed discourse of protection, these bills have largely targeted trans youth, barring them from accessing various forms of gender-affirmative care, especially healthcare. In one of the more visibly severe moves, in February 2022, the state

Introduction: Trans Antagonisms and Beauvoir

of Texas's governor, Gregg Abbott, formally defined standard practices of trans-affirmative healthcare for people under the age of 18 as child abuse. Although met with fierce opposition, in June 2023, Abbott signed into a law a bill that bars trans kids from getting puberty blockers and hormone therapies, joining 17 other states that ban trans people under the age of 18 from accessing affirmative healthcare, even with parental or guardian support.

These legislative moves, while a concerted effort of a faction of Republicans in the US, are backed by social commentators and have gained traction among the general public. In 2021, two-thirds of Americans, across all political ideologies and of every age group, were opposed to legislation that infringed upon the rights of transgender people (Loffman, 2021). By 2023, the landscape had drastically changed. While most Americans still favor protecting transgender people from formal discrimination in jobs and housing, there is now much at play that contradicts this general opinion: 43 percent of Americans now support laws that criminalize trans-affirmative healthcare for minors, a 15-percentage point increase in just two years (Santhanam, 2023). As many as 41 percent of Americans believe it should be illegal for government-funded schools to teach about gender identity in elementary classes (Pew Research, 2022). Around 58 percent of Americans believe that trans athletes must compete on teams that match their sex assigned at birth. There is very little public support for requiring health insurance to cover medical care for gender transitions. And there is growing belief in the view that gender is determined by sex at birth. The emergence of these more widespread public opinions compromises the social conditions that make it possible to live as a trans person. In a social context in which you cannot learn about people like you, in which you cannot play with others as you are, in which you cannot receive and are not supported in receiving care to support your health, the capacity *to be* a trans person in the world is eroded. These emergent social sentiments, then, contribute to an atmosphere that makes trans existence impossible. This reality is compounded by the fact that transgender people face shocking amounts of physical violence in the United States.

Across the Atlantic, there are also notable legislative efforts that erode trans possibilities. In January 2023, under Conservative Prime Minister Rishi Sunak, the British government blocked a Scottish law that would have made it easier for people to change their legal gender. Had the Scottish legislation taken effect, Scotland would have been the first constituent country of the UK to establish a self-identification system for trans people, making it easier for them to change the sex on their birth certificate. Since 2004, the UK has operated according to guidelines established in the Gender Recognition Act, which enables an individual to apply for and receive a birth certificate, or a Gender Recognition Certificate, that correctly identifies who one is, so long as they have received a medical diagnosis for gender dysphoria and have proved themselves capable of living in their "preferred" gender for two years. Scotland's legislation de-medicalized this process, allowing people 16 and older to change their gender on identity documents through self-declaration, thus introducing a system that prioritizes the principle of self-identification. Insofar as the removal of the requirement of medical diagnosis, combined with the fact that the law shortened the amount of time one needs to live in one's gender (from two years to three months for people over the age of 17, and to six months for 16- and 17-year-olds), displaces the power of authority to sanc-

Introduction: Trans Antagonisms and Beauvoir

tion trans existence, the Scottish legislation would have conferred stronger legal and social standing for trans people. In blocking the bill, the British government sent a message about its authority over trans lives, and in the months that followed, proposed further legislative moves that would undermine positive legal and social conditions for trans people. The main target was the Equality Act.

The Equality Act of 2010 not only streamlined anti-discrimination law in the UK, but also expanded it by offering, for the first time, protections against indirect discrimination and direct discrimination in schools, based on gender reassignment. Central to this expansion was a legal redefinition of 'sex.' According to the Equality Act, any transgender person with a Gender Recognition Certificate is of the same sex as a non-transgender person, a move that grants not only parity in legal standing between trans and non-trans people, but formally rejects the claim that transgender people are not *really* who they say they are. In other words, according to the Equality Act, transgender women *are women*, full stop, all the way down to their sex. In April 2023, Tory Minister for Women and Equalities, Kemi Badenoch, proposed to change the legal definition of sex. This change would amend the Equality Act such that 'sex' would be defined exclusively as biological sex, by which the proposed amendment means "sex assigned at birth." In other words, it would legally sanction the gender-critical claim that natal women are *real* women. As chapter 2 shows, and Beauvoir herself already knew, the matter-of-factness of biological sex is not actually a given, but when it is taken to be, as the proposed change by Badenoch purports, biological sex undercuts trans life. The redefinition means a trans woman is not "by sex" a woman, such that the proposal, if it were to become law, would make the exclusion of trans people from sex-segregated or gender-specific public and private services the status quo. Such a redefinition means that, in the UK, no public institution could legally exclude anyone due to their trans identity but could exclude a person based on their legal sex. Proponents of the proposed changes to the Equality Act insist that these changes would be made to secure protections for girls and women, by which they mean, but do not say, *natal* girls and women. Opponents insist that such moves, if codified into law, clear the way for the discrimination, harassment, and marginalization of trans people at structural and social levels.

While the law has not yet changed, such legislative proposals are consistent with the gender-critical sentiments that have secured a foothold in the UK. Indeed, in June 2024, Sunak pledged to redefine biological sex to "protect" girls and women if he is reelected. Gender-critical views emerged in the public in new ways in 2018 after a proposal to reform the 2004 Gender Recognition Act (GRA) was introduced, a reform that would have prioritized the principle of self-identification, making it easier for transgender people, and transgender women in particular, to have their gender formally recognized. As with the history of feminism in the United States, gender-critical views in the UK had, amongst non-trans women who called themselves feminists, been around since at least the 1970s. But it was not until this proposed reform that a large and vocal group of gender-critical individuals and organizations surfaced. Stock, a professor of philosophy at the University of Sussex until 2021, has been one of the most visible, advocating for laws that define womanhood on the basis of biological sex and, in turn, that deny that trans women are real women. At the time of the 2018 proposed reform to the GRA, in an interview with a local newspaper, Stock asserted:

Introduction: Trans Antagonisms and Beauvoir

> many trans women are still males with male genitalia, many are sexually attracted to females, and they should not be in places where females undress or sleep in a completely unrestricted way ... Trans women are biologically male, and though most are law-abiding, some small proportion are not. There is a general social need to continue to protect females in communal female-only spaces from the possibility of male violence. (Braidwood, 2018)

These statements went viral on Twitter and were met with significant criticism. Stock's persistent public avowal of such a view brought her under intense scrutiny and opposition by those who affirm trans existence on trans terms. She claimed her freedom of speech was being compromised. Her opposition claimed her views are exclusionary of trans people and therefore created hostile conditions for their lives, a point that was particularly charged for trans students at the University of Sussex. Why should Stock's freedom of speech trump their right to exist? Why is the university willing to tolerate hostile views about trans people being pushed by their faculty, especially in ways and forums that are publicly and politically influential? Why should trans students have to debate and defend their existence to their professor? Stock claims her views are not trans exclusionary but rooted in philosophical argumentation over the validity of gender identity. Her opponents refuse the move, arguing instead that views that deny trans women are women or that insist that biological sex determines gender are rooted in the denial that trans people are who they say they are. That denial is taken to be an aggressive exclusion of trans people from participating in life *as trans people*.

The various manifestations of the broader gender-critical discourse work adjacent to and sometimes directly in concert with conservative politicians who target trans existence. Although not necessarily representative of most people in the UK or US, their circulation is undeniably impactful. Legislative proposals have the clear capacity to erode legal protections for trans people, and they do so by deploying so-called commonsense views about sex against trans existence. The outcome of such a legal landscape is a society in which discrimination against and exclusion of trans people *as trans people* is rendered a *non-issue*. The visibility and circulation of gender-critical discourse creates a social landscape that not only questions, but also undermines, the legitimacy of being transgender. The permissibility of gender-critical discourse is often framed only as an issue of free speech and matter of philosophical debate, but there is an important ethical issue at stake in its circulation. By insisting that trans women are not *real* women, gender-critical discourse undercuts the affirmative view that transgender people are who they say they are and that, because they are who they say they are, everyone should recognize and respect trans people on the basis of their own self-definitions. In effect, the gender-critical insistence justifies the conservative political maneuvers being made against trans people. If trans women are not women, if no trans person is who they say they are, then there's no need to socially or legally recognize or secure protections for any trans person as a trans person.

The US and the UK are certainly not alone in the presence and insurgence of **trans antagonisms**, or the constellation of hostile forces that undermine trans life here and now, and the possibility for trans existence in the future. But whereas several other Western nations work to continue to advance trans rights, the US and the UK continue to target and undermine them. As agenda-setting actors in the global political stage, their respective fixations on and pursuits of anti-trans

Introduction: Trans Antagonisms and Beauvoir

policies and beliefs matter. They are influential. Take, for instance, the fact that in March 2023 the World Athletics Council, the global governing body of sport, which is deeply influenced by the politics and interests of Western nations, banned trans women from competing in women's sports during the Summer 2024 Olympics. So, although hostilities toward and discrimination against transgender people are neither exclusive to the US or the UK, nor apparent only in Western nations, their manifestations in these particular places are evidence of a particular brand of trans antagonism characteristic of anti-trans sentiments in Western nations. These sentiments align the allegedly more progressive West with countries that are presumed to be "backward" when it comes to social inclusion and acceptance of gender and sexual minorities. Ultimately, these two contexts are instructive to focus on, even if trans antagonisms exist elsewhere in distinct ways. At the same time, because the contemporary landscape of trans antagonisms in Western democratic nations is aligned with the rise of far-right, fascist politics that bolster white nationalism, attention to the anti-trans forces in these contexts elucidates how such racist political movements target categories and realities of sex and gender as a primary means of control. The regulation of categories of sex and gender, as well as womanhood, has long been central to the establishment of white supremacy (Davis, 1981; Hartman, 1997; Lugones, 2007; Snorton, 2017); contemporary trans antagonisms are the latest iteration.

Legislative actions or proposals of the kind just mentioned, and gender-critical beliefs, are extreme manifestations of trans antagonisms. Trans antagonisms manifest in more mundane, less extreme, and subtle ways, however. There are collective habits and norms, including beliefs about what sex and gender are, which operate to invalidate, delegitimize, and thus erode trans existence and possibility. It is important, then, not to characterize trans antagonism as only a form of extremism. As chapter 1 will show in detail, Beauvoir's account of becoming a woman makes very clear that patriarchal injustices are baked into our everyday lives not in sensational ways, but through how others treat us. For this reason, this book does not just speak back to legislation and discourse that are overtly trans exclusionary. This book also speaks to taken-for-granted social practices that invalidate and deny trans existence. Focusing first on the extreme forms of antagonisms is one way to begin to suss out how trans antagonisms operate today and what their underlying commitments are.

The Harm of Trans Antagonisms

This book operates from the premise that trans antagonisms are transphobic and therefore harmful to trans people. Given that trans antagonisms claim to operate from the values of care, protection, and freedom, it is worth offering an initial outline of this driving premise. In mainstream terms, transphobia refers to negative, prejudicial, or hostile attitudes or actions toward transgender people. This definition of transphobia suggests that formal, or legalistic, discrimination against transgender people, as well as social stigma and marginalization, is rooted in conscious or unconscious fear, hate, or disgust. While it is certainly the case that phobias are more generally defined in relation to such affective dispositions, this conception of transphobia tends to overly individualize and pathologize its reality. As opposed to understanding **transphobia** as a normalized and systemic reality, one woven into the social fabric such that it comprises the status quo, the mainstream conception fashions transphobia as a phenomenon enacted only by

Introduction: Trans Antagonisms and Beauvoir

a few "bad apples." On this definition of transphobia, the harm emerges from individual actors who have bad feelings about trans people and, as a result, take hostile actions against them, usually in the form of physical violence. Anyone who does not consciously harbor or act on such bad feelings is not transphobic and so not enacting harm against trans people.

Philosopher Talia Bettcher (2006) proposes another definition, one that will be returned to later in greater detail. For Bettcher, there is a basic kind of transphobia, which she names the **Basic denial of authenticity** (BDA). At its core, BDA is a way of knowing that insists that the truth of a person's gender is to be determined by genitalia, and the expectation is that this truth can be read or known by others through an individual's gender presentation. Concretely, this means that if, when walking down the street, there is someone whose gender presentation reads as feminine, most will, without hesitation, assume and expect not only that this person is a woman, but will also assume and expect, often unconsciously, to know something about her genital status. If this person is a woman, but somehow it is found out that she does not have the "correct" genitals (which usually happens through violent, forced exposure), at the very least the truth of who "she" is will be thrown into question, but most likely invalidated. In other words, when her genital status is exposed, that she is a woman will be denied. No matter her gender presentation and self-identification, she will not be recognized as a real woman. Or, to put it more succinctly, as Bettcher does, the "identification of sex with genital status is often what overrides the self-identities of trans people" and thus denies trans people's claims about who they are (2009, p. 108).

Ultimately, what BDA does is override the first-person claims of trans people by conferring "reality" and "truth" to genital status. The harm of BDA is that by imposing and enforcing the view that genitalia are the "truth" of one's gender, trans people are taken to be pretenders, or deceivers, or are denied outright the chance to be who they say they are. That denial can take the form of suspicion or misrecognition – for instance, a trans woman is seen as and understood to be "really a man" – or the denial can take the form of physical violence. The harm of this basic form of transphobia is the refusal or denial of trans people's self-identifications. When people deny that a trans person is who they say they are, that trans person is erased from existence, even if they are not subject to physical violence. Although, certainly, the severity of the harm depends on the form and situation in which the denial is lived, the harm, which occurs *on the basis of an alleged truth about genital status*, is first and foremost *existential*. It is a matter of how we live individually and collectively and how we take responsibility for the ways we live our lives with others. It is a harm that need not be overt but can be found in commonly held beliefs and practices about what it is to be a woman or a man. As will be discussed throughout this book, that the harm is existential highlights that human existence is a social existence – not, as gender-critical views claim, biological.

Accordingly, BDA can be understood to be at the heart of the contemporary legislation and gender-critical views insofar as both operate from the premise that biological sex is what makes one a "real" woman or man, a premise that is being enforced, both legislatively and ideologically. Indeed, many of the legislative measures in the US, for instance, *ban* trans existence altogether by insisting on the metaphysical truth of biological sex, which opens pathways for the rejection and exclusion of trans people in society more generally. In effect, if who trans people say they are is not real, then who trans people are need not be recognized or respected. Even

Introduction: Trans Antagonisms and Beauvoir

more perniciously, such a view suggests that trans existence should not be supported or affirmed because it is a corrupt way to be. For trans people, the consequence is a world in which being trans is taken to be fundamentally illegitimate. This framing of trans existence is the justification that fuels actions, efforts, and the persistence of sentiments that deauthorize and impoverish, if not altogether eradicate, trans life. There are damaging personal, social, and material outcomes for trans people that follow. The possibility to exist, to have life chances, is diminished.

For the Sake of Girls and Women

The gender-critical insistence is that the lives of non-trans women are the ones being compromised today by trans activism. The author of the Harry Potter series (Rowling, 2020a) captures this claim in a controversial blog post from June 10, 2020, when she writes that the *real* harm in today's landscape of gender politics is that trans activism is "seeking to erode 'woman' as a political and biological class and offering cover to predators like few before it." On this view, trans activists commit and promote violence against (non-trans) women. Yet the violence is not primarily physical; it is 'woman,' as a category, that is violated. Gender-critical feminists want to save the category 'woman' from trans activism, to define 'woman' as a particular kind of category that excludes and denies the possibility of all trans existence. Consequently, the categorical defense of 'woman' does not just rule out trans girls and women as girls and women, but also rejects that trans boys and men are who they say they are. The aim, gender-critical feminists claim, is to protect "natal women," to make sure their lives are not erased, silenced, or subject to further violation.

There is a history animated in such moves to save and protect 'woman.' Decades of feminist scholarship have shown that the category is not a neutral one, but a site in which struggles for power have played out. It has long been carved out and preserved as one that only names white, property-owning, heterosexual women. Changes in social and political landscapes that threaten 'woman,' that seek to expand who is named by this category and what it means, have historically been met by efforts to keep 'woman' as property of the ruling class. What is at stake is therefore a matter of power, of who gets to control meaning and the material conditions of 'woman.' It is not just a matter of gender, it is a matter of power, of historical legacies of power and domination that are realized through regulating womanhood. The struggle to secure 'woman' as a trans exclusive category for the sake of women as "a political and biological class" is what makes a philosophical consideration of 'woman' relevant to the contemporary politics of trans existence. After all, to reiterate Beauvoir's motivating question in *The Second Sex*, what is a woman anyway? Far from an intellectual exercise, how the question is answered matters politically and materially; it is about the conditions under which a woman exists and the kind of woman she gets to become. Gender-critical feminists know this too, or else they wouldn't insist on saving 'woman' from trans women.

In *The Second Sex*, Beauvoir debunks myths about 'woman,' about who she is, and shows what it does to a human being to become a woman. Beauvoir describes at great length that becoming a woman has something, but nothing essential or natural, to do with physiological difference, which she argues is a *patriarchal conception* of 'woman' and therefore an oppressive one. Gender-critical readings of Beauvoir tend to ignore or misread this latter dimension of her work, and instead focus only

Introduction: Trans Antagonisms and Beauvoir

on the fact that Beauvoir did not deny a relation between becoming a woman and bodily differences. Yet, as each chapter of this book will show, Beauvoir's understanding of this relation was not essential – rather, she urged us to see patriarchal oppression as codifying biological essentialism. The move to demarcate 'woman' as a biological category is, Beauvoir argues, a product of patriarchy, and such a view is a condition of patriarchal oppression and violence against women. From a Beauvoirian perspective, then, if there is anyone being duped today, it would be those who adopt gender-critical views, not those of us who embrace trans existence. As a social destiny, becoming a woman is created by the imposition of and socialization into certain human-made expectations, values, and norms. 'Woman' could be done differently. This reading of Beauvoir does not suggest she is offering an account of womanhood as biological, as a social construction, or as a gender identity. Indeed, as will be discussed later in the book, Beauvoir's account of becoming a woman also encourages us to see the limitations and problems of gender identity discourse. However, contra the gender-critical dismissal of gender identity, a Beauvoirian account that challenges gender identity does not lead to the rejection of trans existence as valid. The reading of "becoming a woman" advanced in this book shows that such becoming is experiential.

This reading of Beauvoir is not merely an intellectual exercise. It is about a struggle for meaning and such a struggle is not without concrete, material implications. How 'woman' is understood, who gets to inhabit 'woman,' and how and what 'woman' is allowed to become or unbecome is about what kind of world we ought to make and how we ought to live in it with others. It is a matter of what possibilities we allow or deny to ourselves and to others. It is a matter of how life chances and possibilities are created and distributed.

I
Becoming a Woman

When my mom gave birth to me, she didn't know how the doctor would categorize me. She didn't know if on the crib in the hospital nursery there would be a celebratory sign marking me as a girl or as a boy. She didn't know what information would populate my birth certificate. In the early 1980s in the United States, advanced ultrasound technology wasn't widely available, so the pressure "to know" what genitalia I would have didn't exist yet. There wasn't a baby shower since, at that time in the US, baby showers were reserved for the first-born of the family and I was the second. Gender reveals were not yet the outrageous trend they are today. Despite these historical differences, meaning was still being attached to my existence, in advance of my existence. Surrounding my mom's pregnancy were social myths – about how low or high her belly was, about her food cravings – that circulated as signs of what I was going to be.

My parents still had "girl" and "boy" names ready to go once they knew "what" I was. My mom's naming powers were vetoed by my dad after she proposed they name me Ruby, a name that was, at the time at least, unconventional. My dad preferred names that were very of the time: Megan or Eric. Turns out, based on what they were told about me once I did exist outside of the womb, I became Megan, one of the most popular names for girls in the US in the 1980s (my older sister, Heather, had another one of those names).

Once I did exist in the world, the gendered meanings came in full force, authoritatively and subliminally, both different ways in which the dominant meanings of the social fabric ushered me into a particular gendered existence. There was the performative utterance of the doctor – "It's a girl!" – which began my existence *as a girl*. While usually taken to be an objective matter-of-fact statement, feminist thinkers have shown that such a statement doesn't just name a reality but makes the reality itself. I *became* a girl because I was named one. I wasn't named one arbitrarily, of course. There was a convention, a tradition, a history in place that made it common sense that at birth, I was clearly, obviously, a girl. No one in that hospital room was going to say otherwise; it would've been nonsense. My birth certificate was made, and on it there was a big F, a formal decree of what I was. Beyond these formalities, there was all the social stuff – the flurry of ways people, including my parents, talked to and about me, held me, clothed me, and bought toys for me. Even if they didn't know it, or even if they didn't mean to, there was an avalanche of expectations in place about what I was made of. I was to be sugar and spice and everything nice. Still to this day, I have a vivid recollection of a kitschy, wooden sign with that nursery rhyme on it. It wasn't for me. It was given to my older sister, but the message was clear. Throughout my childhood, the meanings at work in my life became more complex. My parents did not explicitly raise me to be everything nice, or to be seen and not heard. I grew up playing soccer with my mom as my coach. My dad inspired an early fascination with Volkswagen cars, which he encouraged. I played in the dirt and got into trouble with my sister. I wasn't forced to wear dresses, but they were most often the option available. And yet, still, my childhood was characterized by so many things typical of a white girl in the United States in the 1980s, not to mention that the expectations and values of how I should be were the air that I breathed. As a result, their impact on who I became was inevitable.

When Beauvoir describes the lived experience of becoming a woman, she begins with an account of childhood that underscores the constitutive weight of the social atmosphere on shaping who an individual becomes. What's "in the air" around us as we come into our existence is central to who we become. For Beauvoir, there is no blueprint for a child's existence that comes from their genitalia, which is to say that genitalia *themselves* don't determine who one is. Rather, a child's existence is, Beauvoir claims, a result of how their bodily existence is mediated. That sexual difference means anything at all about who we are is a human mediation. A girl, or boy, wouldn't take their genitalia to have any existential significance without this mediation, without the conferral of meaning. A girl, then, is a girl not strictly because of her genitalia or other physiological differences, but because of how her embodied existence unfolds and is taken up in a given context. It is not her body that dictates who she is. Who she becomes is a matter of her bodily relationality in the world with others. Or, as Beauvoir puts it, the girl's "vocation [as a woman] is imperiously breathed into her from the first years of her life" (2010, p. 283). This point leads back to the opening sentence of her account of lived experience: "One is not born, but rather becomes, a woman" (1949b, p. 13).

Usually, when I talk with students about Beauvoir's insistence that the external world is inextricable from the reality of being a woman – which is to say, no one is simply born destined to be a woman – they are quick to jump to the seemingly reliable distinction between nature and nurture. She must be, my students insist, making a point about the significance of nurture. They're not entirely wrong. Beauvoir is making a case that there is a very deep socialization that those who are girls undergo. In *The Second Sex*, she offers us pages and pages replete with details about how parents and adults intervene in children's lives in ways that differentiate girls from boys. Girls are given toys and treated in ways that make them passive, they are told and taught to be pretty and giving, as to focus on doing so is a matter of their worth. Girls are given certain clothes, told to carry themselves a certain way, are taught to do certain tasks while they are barred from others, and are expected to serve others. Ultimately, Beauvoir claims, what adults do is expect that girls accomplish femininity. In fact, she even goes so far as to say adults demand this of girls. This demand is the air girls breathe and it is vital to their becoming women.

To say that the girl's existence is a just matter of nurture would contradict and oversimplify Beauvoir's commitments about human existence. For Beauvoir, our development *is* social; it does depend on the context in which we live out our lives. It does depend on how others perceive and treat us. It is, then, "nurture." But it's not just that. There are dimensions of our existence that are inevitable, such as the reality that there are others in the world or that humans, as a species, have basic needs that must be met to stay alive. The term Beauvoir gives this dimension of existence is **facticity**, and central to this dimension is the body, not as biologically determinative, but in the sense that every subject is bodily, and it is as bodily beings that we have the possibility for existence in the first place. But, before you are quick to think this contradicts the point just made about Beauvoir insisting that genitalia or other reproductive differences do not bear any existential significance, it is important to remember that her point is not that bodies do not matter, but that existence doesn't boil down to reproductive physiological differences. Embodiment is, for Beauvoir, about so much more than our reproductive organs. Embodiment is about the relation between body and world. It is that how we are touched, who we are touched by, how we move, whether we're able to, what we desire, are constitutive features of our bodily existence. But that doesn't mean it's all "nurture" either. Rather, for her, it is at the entanglement of 'nature' and 'nurture' that we come into existence. Yet these categories aren't Beauvoir's terms and using them to understand her work is misleading. The fault of relying on "nurture" is that it doesn't give any agency to an individual to shape her life, so, although a girl is deeply reared into becoming a woman, it is also, Beauvoir says, a project she undertakes for herself too. Ultimately, Beauvoir doesn't want to pin down an origin in either side of the nature or nurture debate. She insists instead that we deal with the **ambiguity** of our existence, that we are never just purely bodies or purely determined from the world imposing itself on us. Rather than locating the origin of the truth of our lives in either nature or nurture, Beauvoir says we must accept that we are always both, that we cannot escape that we have bodily differences and yet we cannot escape the fact that those differences are *always* lived and experientially constituted in a given context that imbues them with meaning.

The intuition my students have about "nurture," however, is more accurately understood if we think about the girl as being socialized to become a woman. In Beauvoir's account, the girl is, without a doubt, deeply socialized to assume her existence as a woman, and as a particular kind of woman, the kind that conforms to patriarchal ideology. Indeed, for Beauvoir, there's no doubt that in childhood there is significant external demand on a girl to become a woman. And so, she most often does. However, it's still an oversimplification to talk about Beauvoir's account as one of socialization. She doesn't simply describe women's socialization from birth to adulthood. That is not the point of her project. Instead, "Beauvoir offers us a rich, critical account of the girl's relentless encounter with the norms and material conditions of femininity in language, in institutions, and in embodied practices" (Mann, 2017, p. 52). In doing so, Beauvoir shows how girls are trained to be passive, to experience objectification as commonplace, to prioritize the values and lives of boys and men over themselves, and to be complicit in their own subordination. The point Beauvoir makes is that a girl's entire trajectory from childhood to adulthood is one in which her existence is mutilated. Beauvoir doesn't account for that mutilation as primarily physical, though it could be. Her account is one of the existential mutilation of being socialized into femininity, which is, for Beauvoir, *the* injustice of patriarchy. Such mutilation steals from the girl the capacity to make her life and the world in ways not overdetermined by the demands of the conventions that saturate the air she breathes.

It can be said, then, that my own becoming as a girl was inaugurated by the very early intervention of others in my existence, not by my body itself. The doctor's declaration, the name my parents chose, the marker on my birth certificate, and the avalanche of expectations about what it was to be a white girl in the world that ensued were how my existence as a girl got off the ground. These expectations were subtle, aggressive, explicit, and tacit. They were not merely scripted onto me, though. I was not a passive object made into someone by others. Rather, I came to take up and grasp my bodily self in relation to the demands and expectations of others. I took up some of these demands and expectations without question. Others I protested against. Some hurt – like the time I was bullied by peers for being too flat-chested to be pretty (ironically, years later, I was told I stuffed my bra, which I didn't want to wear but did anyway). Or, like the time I was called a "lezzie" for holding hands with a girl in the playground (turns out, for a time at least, I would become one). Other expectations didn't hurt. The time my sister and I modeled for a popular girls' clothing store at the local mall was peak recognition; it signaled that I met standards of feminine beauty – white, blonde, thin. But, no matter how these expectations felt to me, so long as I complied or corrected myself when I failed, I was made legible as a future woman through them. In other words, these expectations that were set out for me, that were assumed for me, laid out my social destiny as a woman. Nothing inside of me predetermined that I would become a woman. I was to become a woman because of how I was situated in the world I was thrown into. And I was to become not just a woman, but a passive, feminine woman who existed *for men* – what Beauvoir calls a **relative existence**. As Beauvoir puts it in the second sentence of Volume II of *The Second Sex*, the one right after the most famous sentence: "No biological, psychic, or economic destiny defines the figure that the human female takes on in society; it is civilization as a whole that elaborates this intermediary product between the male and the eunuch that is called feminine" (2010, p. 283).

In many ways, it was *almost* inevitable that I would become a woman. As a white, American, middle-class child, the norms of gender were made for me to inhabit. And the demand for me to do so was ontologically heavy, meaning they weighed on and overwhelmed my existence in subtle and not so subtle ways. Volume II of *The Second Sex* is where Beauvoir describes the lived experience of that becoming. She shows how heavy the demands of others are on childhood and adolescence, such that it's practically impossible for a girl to become otherwise. That impossibility is compounded by what she uncovers in Volume I – namely, that history, myths, and dominant discourses also conspire to limit the possibilities for becoming. This is how social expectations and traditions become quasi-destiny. Even though Beauvoir claims human beings are not predetermined by anything, she also understands that we can be weighed down by the conferral of meaning, by the movement of history, by the norms and values that are taken for granted because they govern our lives in significant ways. The moment I was named a girl, the moment I was marked as F, through all the experiences of expectation, I was, Beauvoir suggests, doomed to become a relative, subordinated existence.

The social destiny of becoming a woman is, on Beauvoir's account, a forceful blueprint for my existence, predetermined in advance of knowing who I am or how I desire to be in the world. It is a matter of how the conventions, values, and expectations, fabrications of the sociopolitical context in which I live, are imposed on me, and a matter of how I negotiate them, live them out in my relations with others and with myself, and come to embody them physically and psychically. The heavy-handedness is how this socially produced, and thus contingent, reality is lived as a destiny. That I, and others designated F at birth, mostly become women subjected to patriarchal norms is not because we *are really* women; it is a result of how overwhelming those norms are. To be a woman is, for Beauvoir, to assume a very particular kind of existence that is neither natural nor inevitable; it is a matter of how we embody and negotiate the possibilities of the concrete situation in which we live.

The Sex–Gender Distinction

The shaping of possibility is something that Stock draws attention to in her presentation of Beauvoir in *Material Girls*. Stock points out that Beauvoir brings to light "how, as the female infant turns into the girl turns into the woman, she's increasingly exposed to images and stereotypes concerning how she *should* behave, think and feel" (Stock, 2021, p. 13). These prescriptions are really a matter of "something called 'femininity,'" which, as Stock notes, Beauvoir understood to serve the interests of men (2021, p. 13). Stock doesn't take issue with this dimension of Beauvoir's account. What Stock does take issue with is how scholars have interpreted Beauvoir's distinction between being and becoming in her famous sentence. For Stock, the sentence "has been taken up enthusiastically to convey the idea that being a woman is not the same as being born biologically female" (2021, p. 12). In other words, Stock doesn't disagree with Beauvoir's account of the harms of femininity as they are imposed on women (who were girls who were female infants); Stock believes Beauvoir's famous sentence has been erroneously interpreted.

More specifically, Stock claims that scholars in "the 1960s, 70s, and 80s . . . newly formed Women's Studies departments in universities" turned Beauvoir's work into something she never intended: an account of gender (2021, p. 13). Or, as Stock puts it, by (mis)interpreting the famous sentence "[t]he conceptual distinction between 'sex' and 'gender' was born" (2021, p. 14). This interpretation was indicative of a moment in feminist theorizing in which "it was important to think of gender ... as purely social, without foundation in biological generalisations about women and men" (2021, p. 13). This moment is an important one in the history of feminist thought. As a challenge to the dominant understanding of differences between women and men, this conceptual distinction afforded feminists a way to address patriarchal ideology. So, Stock is right: Beauvoir was a key resource for scholars in creating a distinction between sex as biological and gender as social. People might be born with genital and reproductive differences, but one becomes feminine or masculine. This maps sex onto being and gender onto becoming, which, for Stock, incorrectly guides subsequent interpretations of Beauvoir. With this reading, the famous sentence is read as an articulation of the **sex–gender distinction**. There were, Stock insists, troubling ramifications of this reading of Beauvoir. "In the decades that followed, some feminist commentators moved beyond this distinction to a much more radical position," Stock writes:

> They started approvingly to interpret de Beauvoir as having meant that womanhood itself is essentially social not biological: not a matter of being female but rather a matter of having projected on to you, and perhaps also internalising, the restrictive social expectations, stereotypes, and norms of femininity. They took women and girls to be, by definition, the set of people who have a feminine "social role" projected upon them. (2021, p. 14)

It is true that the sex–gender distinction became an important conceptual framework for feminist scholars in the 1970s. The distinction was largely an appropriation of psychologist Robert Stoller's distinction between sex as referring to biological traits and gender as referring to the social roles of femininity or masculinity, a distinction he made to explain the reality of transsexuality. While the ethics of Stoller's research and treatment of transsexual people is problematic, feminist scholars took to the distinction, and to the concept of gender in particular, to highlight that women's inferior social and political status is not biological, but a result of the social roles they are socialized into and expected to take up. That is, although there may be biological differences, those differences are not why women have an inferior status. It is not the reality of sex, but the reality of gender that is the problem. In short, the concept of gender draws attention to how the realm of the social is the locus of oppression.

The feminist turn to the sex–gender distinction has been the site of much debate amongst feminist scholars since its appropriation. It has been argued that it fails to explain gender differences, that it fails to diagnose the nature of women's subordination, and that it takes gender to be real and descriptive as opposed to fictive and prescriptive. Beauvoir's famous sentence has been along for the ride the entire time. For this reason, Stock is correct that the famous sentence has been a site from which feminist scholars account for, insist on, and justify the distinction itself. But not all readings of Beauvoir map the sex–gender distinction onto her famous sentence. In fact, one of the most prominent critiques of this reading of Beauvoir comes from those of us who read Beauvoir as a phenomenologist, as opposed to a social constructionist (Moi, 2001; Heinämaa, 2003; Bergoffen, 2017; Burke, 2017; Mann, 2017). A social constructionist interpretation would highlight that constructed gender roles are imposed onto a sexed individual. In contrast, reading Beauvoir as a phenomenologist – a particular kind of philosopher attentive to lived, embodied experience – means acknowledging that embodied situations and social realities are both experientially constituted. This critique is not one Stock considers. In fact, her concern with the interpretation of Beauvoir's

Becoming a Woman

sentence as a formulation of the sex–gender distinction is not even about how Beauvoir understands the reality of becoming a woman.

For Stock, the significance of, and trouble with, the sex–gender interpretation of Beauvoir is not that it gets Beauvoir's philosophical commitments wrong. It's that it pushes a trans inclusive conception of womanhood. "It looks like a consequence of this view that – at least potentially," Stock writes, "being a woman doesn't require being female, nor being a man, being male ... this apparently opens up the possibility of a trans woman counting as a woman – quite literally – as long as she occupies a feminine social role just as other women do" (2021, p. 14). This "consequence" of reading Beauvoir's famous sentence is more important to Stock than what Beauvoir actually meant in positing the distinction between being and becoming. Stock worries about thinking that encourages, even requires, us to recognize trans women as women, full stop. Indeed, Stock states that what Beauvoir meant is moot, and yet Stock goes on to state, but not account for, the fact that she doesn't think Beauvoir "intended the conceptual separation of being female from womanhood" (Stock, 2021, p. 14). Later, in the chapter "What Makes a Woman," Stock finally gives us a bit more insight into her reading of Beauvoir:

> The fact that in *The Second Sex* de Beauvoir was fairly obviously talking only about females and their involuntary encounters with a social system subjecting them to impossible ideals of femininity from birth seems mostly ignored. De Beauvoir wasn't talking about males who decide after puberty to radically alter their bodies artificially, and nor would she have excluded from the purview of her claims any trans man who did similar. Still, whatever the case, her quote has found new life in a modern context. (Stock, 2021, p. 163)

Becoming a Woman

For readers less familiar with *The Second Sex*, Stock is referring to Beauvoir's description of becoming a woman in Volume II. Stock's claim about what's "fairly obvious" isn't necessarily wrong. Beauvoir is not describing trans experience. She is giving us a very specific account of a certain kind of "becoming a woman" – it is "fairly obviously" not a trans experience. This does not, however, mean, as Stock seems to want it to, that uptakes of Beauvoir in the "modern context" are therefore wrong to suggest that there is not a necessary biological immutability to our existence such that being a woman is a natural, material reality.

One trouble with Stock's presentation of Beauvoir is that Stock doesn't offer evidence for her reading or account for what Beauvoir meant. Stock assumes that Beauvoir agrees that there is a reality of sex that has an inevitable relation to 'woman.' Given Beauvoir's prominence as a feminist philosopher, and Stock's insistence that Beauvoir has been wrongly interpreted, it is curious that Stock, in a chapter on "the woman question" – the very question that motivates Beauvoir's inquiry – doesn't explain what Beauvoir actually did mean in *The Second Sex*. If everyone is wrong about Beauvoir, on what, if any, grounds is Stock right?

On the one hand, it is anachronistic to find the sex–gender distinction in Beauvoir's work. On the other hand, her philosophical commitments about embodiment refuse such conceptual distinction. Moreover, I also believe that Beauvoir's account is not about trans experience; she describes a very specific kind of becoming of female infants, who become girls, who become women, and who are subjected to norms of femininity that, in Beauvoir's words, mutilate their existence. However, Stock resists the born–becoming/sex–gender reading of Beauvoir for very different reasons than I do. Stock is interested in retaining a conception of 'woman' as necessarily bound to biological sex, the latter of which she understands to be a natural, material reality. In effect, for Stock, 'woman' is also a natural phenomenon insofar as it follows from the immutable material of sex. Stock presents the idea but does not offer evidence that Beauvoir holds a compatible view. Stock's presentation of Beauvoir echoes across gender-critical turns to Beauvoir, including Lawford-Smith's (2022, 2023) reading of Beauvoir.

The gender-critical insistence on the truth of biological sex as real ground for being a woman is a "commonsense" view. That is, the assumption that most people make about the existence of women is that they form a biological group bound together on the basis of a particular physiology – that is, in sex. To put it another way, the common-sense view is that, regardless of any differences among those who are women, what makes one a woman is a natural fact, a meaning fixed in the nature of being female. For Beauvoir, the common-sense understanding of 'woman,' and of any other phenomenon, needs to be thoroughly investigated. As is the case for all phenomenologists, it is necessary to subject the **natural attitude** to critical analysis. The natural attitude refers to our everyday, ordinary perception, or what we take for granted. It is that which we see and experience as a matter of fact, as "just the way things are." The natural attitude is a perspective that is generally not recognized or experienced as a perspective. While it isn't inherently bad, the natural attitude needs critical reflection. In the absence of such reflection, our perception, experience, and knowledge of the world is laced in a profound *naïveté*. It is the task of a phenomenologist to expose and engage the natural attitude, not to accept it as fact. It is from this methodological starting point that Beauvoir writes *The Second Sex*, and critically investigates what a woman is, including what the relationship between 'woman' and 'female' is. In other words, she doesn't set out to defend the common-sense view. She investigates its formation and exposes what we take for granted to be true. We cannot, in Beauvoir's view, just accept that 'sex' exists as the truth of who we are – nor can we accept that 'female' and 'woman' have any essential relationship. We must understand both the meaning and condition of emergence of this natural attitude or common-sense view.

Accordingly, the insistence on the natural, necessary relation between 'female' and 'woman' is where the gender-critical turn to Beauvoir gets it wrong. While the next chapter will unpack Beauvoir's understanding of this relation, it is first important to consider her distinction between the philosophical contexts of 'born' and 'becoming' in relation to the reality of women's existence. Doing so shows that Beauvoir does not posit a sex–gender distinction, but also that she takes 'woman' to be a particular kind of becoming, one that is highly specific and a seemingly fixed existence.

On Being and Becoming

As discussed in the Introduction, in the history of Western philosophy, there is a classic distinction between being and becoming, both of which are terms that refer to metaphysical commitments about the nature of phenomena. Being refers to an eternal, unchanging essence, while becoming refers to the changing, shifting character of existence. Those who claim that the nature of existence is being believe that there is a predetermined way things are, a fixed human nature such that no matter what happens or what the circumstances are, there is just a way humans are. Name changes, hormone therapy, body modifications, or feelings and ideas about one's lived experience can't change that. Nothing alters one's being; it just always is the case. In contrast, those who claim that the nature of existence is becoming do not believe in a predetermined destiny or fixed essence; if there is a way things are, it is because they have become this way because of various forces. On this view, there is no human nature as such, no pre-given truth about who we are or how we act; the reality of what it means to be human is forged. That there are human beings called women would, then, be understood as a reality emergent from and a consequence of human actions, those of others in the past and in the present, as well as our own.

It seems obvious that Beauvoir draws on the distinction between being and becoming in her famous sentence. She makes it very clear that 'woman' is not a pre-given, natural reality when she asserts, "One is *not* born . . . a woman" (1949b, p. 13; emphasis mine). 'Woman' is not being. Beauvoir is, however, accounting for much more than the contingent truth of the reality of women when she claims, "One . . . *becomes* a woman" (1949b, p. 13; emphasis mine). She devotes hundreds of pages to a description of the experiences central to this becoming not only to show us how one's existence as a woman is experientially constituted, but also to make a claim about the *kind* of becoming "becoming a woman" is. In my view, Beauvoir's description of the lived experience discloses that becoming a woman is, paradoxically, a fixing of existence that is dynamic to one that is static and ahistorical.

Beauvoir's notion of becoming is often read as a claim about what gender is – an inessential, contingently made and lived phenomenon. Such a reading revolves around the born/becoming distinction. Beauvoir's distinction posits that gender, far from being an essential feature of human existence, is not natural, but rather a making of the self. Yet there is another way to read the born–becoming distinction. Bonnie Mann's (2017) reading of Beauvoir suggests that she gives us an account not of what gender is, but rather of what it does. For Mann, Beauvoir's feminist phenomenological account of becoming a woman is an exposition on how the structure of dominance and subordination inheres in norms of gendered existence such that one comes to live an existentially destitute and exploited existence. Although it certainly seems to be the case that Beauvoir says something about what gender is, Mann's point is that Beauvoir is most interested in what becoming does to a subject. When read in this way, becoming is not only an ontological claim – it is also, and perhaps first and foremost, a political claim about the operation of becoming. What Beauvoir describes throughout Volume II is that to become a woman is to be bullied and mutilated into a ready-made value system; it is to come into being through a coercive assignation.

Take, for instance, my own becoming. Beauvoir's question wouldn't be: What am I? The question is: What are the values and expectations about what and who I am, who I should be, *doing to* my existence such that I become a particular *me*, a certain kind of individual? In my case, my life was heavily mediated by white, middle-class, Catholic, American values of girlhood. In Beauvoir's life, it was white, bourgeois, Catholic, French values, values she came to despise and stood in resistance to, intellectually, socially, and politically. The intervention of these values is neither determinate nor superficial; it carries what one could call *ontological weight*, meaning that the intervention or influence of values and conventions shapes who you become in a significant way. Phenomena and experiences that carry ontological weight are a matter of who we become. So, yes, the marker I received on my birth certificate mattered and still does, significantly. That initial naming, that assignment given to me by others, worked on my existence, giving it a contour, a structure that would grip and shape me. And, certainly, there is the undeniable fact of my body, a point which will be the focus of the next chapter. But, as Beauvoir says at the beginning of Volume II, facticity is ensnared with the social from the get-go, one's body is inextricably and deeply linked with a social destiny from the start. That is, the intervention of others was *almost originary*. Who I would become and how I would live my body wasn't open-ended; it was laid out for me by others, by the world I lived in, right from the start.

Beauvoir's remarks about the specification of children as girls (or boys) by adults – that is, their becoming gendered – highlight the coercive mood of the becoming she describes. In her discussion of the apprenticeship the little girl receives, Beauvoir writes:

> women given the care of a little girl are bent on transforming her into women like themselves with zeal and arrogance mixed with resentment. And even the generous mother who sincerely wants the best for her child will, as a rule, think it wiser to make a "true woman" of her, as that is the way she will be accepted by society. (Beauvoir, 2010, pp. 295–6)

Given no choice, the little girl, reared by women, is made into a woman. She becomes a woman because of the intervention by others. The little girl is given orders to obey. For Beauvoir, this intervention is overwhelming. She describes it in this way:

> she is given other little girls as friends . . . books and games are chosen for her that introduce her to her destiny, her ears are filled with the treasures of feminine wisdom, feminine virtues are presented to her, she is taught cooking, sewing, and housework as well as how to dress, how to take care of her personal appearance, charm, and modesty;

> she is dressed in uncomfortable and fancy clothes that she has to take care of, her hair is done in complicated styles, posture is imposed on her: stand up straight, don't walk like a duck; to be graceful, she has to repress spontaneous movements, she is told not to look like a tomboy, strenuous exercise is banned, she is forbidden to fight; in short, she is committed to becoming, like her elders, a servant and an idol. (2010, p. 296)

This intense mediation of a child's life by adults to which Beauvoir draws attention discloses the intentional mood of becoming. The horizon of becoming is not indeterminate but fixed. Initially, it is fixed not by the girl herself, but by adults. Or, as Beauvoir puts it, the girl "is committed to becoming" (2010, p. 296).

What does it mean to be *committed to* becoming? On Beauvoir's terms, it means to be given over to something. As is clear in her account, and as was the case in my life, an infant is given over to the social destiny of becoming a woman by others, especially by parents and other adults who play a role in a child's upbringing. The infant who is deemed a girl by others, and thus committed to the project of becoming a woman, takes up a life inaugurated and structured by the imposition of expectations, values, and meanings by adults. Although it is undoubtedly the case that Beauvoir takes such authorial power as a defining feature of the lives of all children, she is most concerned with what this authorial power does to those who are committed (by others) to becoming women. Beauvoir's description shows that this expression of authorial power – that is, the power to tell a child who she is – is a kind of self-harm. Today, discussions of self-harm are oriented around harm, usually of a physical kind, that an individual does to herself. Beauvoir shows us something else. She shows us how a self, the very formation of a self, can be harmed by how

Becoming a Woman

and who others expect you to be. For the girl, in particular, Beauvoir claims, one is committed to becoming a mutilated self.

In the "Childhood" chapter, in particular, Beauvoir is very clear that the intervention of adults is central to becoming. As Beauvoir describes it, parents and adults apprentice the girl into her impending self-mutilation. The early years of her life are mediated by adults to the extent that she will come to live out the drama that has been laid out for her. Of course, on Beauvoir's account, by adolescence the girl still does not fully accept or submit to the *"assigned destiny,"* but she does not actively refuse it either (Beauvoir, 2010, p. 300; emphasis mine). She lives divided. What does not waiver, however, is the expectation by others, and adults in particular, that she will live out the meanings assigned to her. The expectation is that she will become a woman. At least initially, then, it is not the girl who commits herself to the project of 'woman'; rather, it is adults who commit her. Her mutilation is, to repeat a quote cited earlier, "imperiously breathed into her [by others] from the first years of her life" (2010, p. 283).

That becoming a woman is a mutilation of the self that *begins* with the authorial power of others tells us something important about the character of this becoming. First, the becoming Beauvoir describes is a dominant, taken-for-granted practice in which others name you, in which others tell you who you are. This naming, this telling, or what I referred to above as authorial power, offers a blueprint for your existence. Beauvoir's own philosophical commitments wouldn't lead her to say that this blueprint determines who you are, but her account in *The Second Sex* shows that the blueprint carries weight; it matters a great deal. Second, to become a woman is not to take up an open-ended existence. Rather, it is to be committed to a closed existence. To become a woman is not to become any kind of woman or to become in any way an individual chooses – it is to live a mutilated existence. For Beauvoir, as we will see in the next section, that mutilation is rooted in the closure of one's possibilities. Together, these two features underscore that becoming a woman is a paradox. If becoming is to refer to human existence as indeterminate, then becoming a woman should also be an indeterminate experience. And yet Beauvoir's account shows us otherwise. This is a kind of becoming that is not predetermined by any natural essence, but it is a becoming that lapses into a quasi-determined existence. This becoming aims to guarantee the mutilation of the self, which results from the intense intervention of others into a child's existence. Such a becoming aims to fix one's existence.

Much of Beauvoir's work is characterized by a concern with opposing values and ways of living that foreclose possibilities. In her first philosophical book, *The Ethics of Ambiguity*, published in 1947, Beauvoir associates this disposition with what she calls "the serious world," a kind of existential attitude or manner of taking up and being in the world. Those who live in the serious world, consciously or not, rely on ready-made meanings and values, which, Beauvoir claims, leads to bad faith. That is, their existence is rooted in fleeing their capacity to author the world and themselves. Rather than making values and meanings that respond to the particularity and concreteness of a given situation, an individual who takes up a serious attitude insists on the given, on dominant expectations. In doing so, an individual gives up their freedom; they rely on the "givens" of a world conferred to them by others.

Beauvoir considers the ramifications of "the serious world" on individual and collective existence in her account of childhood and moral development. In *The*

Ethics of Ambiguity, Beauvoir acknowledges that most children are socialized into the serious world by adults. A key characteristic of this socialization is that children are encouraged to submit to being rather than take up an existence of becoming. In other words, children are oriented toward fixed meanings, allowing for the maintenance of a world in which dominant values are upheld and taken for granted as human-made. As a result, such values become naturalized rather than seen for what they are: products of human choices and actions. Children learn, Beauvoir says, to play the "game of being serious" with such importance that they "actually become serious" ([1947] 1976, p. 36). This learning is all a result of the pressure placed on children by adults to adopt the values, images, and scripts that dominate the social order. The result is that children take on an existence, a becoming, that is rooted, paradoxically, in being. It is not a world rooted in a relational freedom where indeterminate possibilities are held open by all. Instead, the serious world fixes certain possibilities as *the only* legitimate possibilities.

It wasn't until after writing *The Ethics of Ambiguity* that Beauvoir discovered the need for a feminist perspective. It is in *The Second Sex* that Beauvoir first understands the serious world as patriarchal. While it is most evident that the serious world aims to fix the girl's existence such that the world weighs down on her, comes at her, comes for her, such that she cannot author the world herself, there is in Beauvoir's description another dimension of the serious world worth paying attention to. Her descriptions of childhood show how the affectations of adults, and parents in particular, are central to gendering of children as boys and girls. She notes time and time again in the "Childhood" chapter that both boys and girls are alienated from their existence by what is assigned to them. They go along with expectations they regret (and Beauvoir insists this is especially the case for girls) because it is what gets children approval and flattery from adults. The almost originary intervention of others, of adults, that inaugurates children's social destiny as a girl or boy is, then, a matter of how fixed, predetermined meaning is given to them by adults. Their becoming, rooted in the serious world, is paradoxically a destiny of being. Children are either girls who become women, or boys who become men, both of which have trajectories outlined and authored for them by others.

Beauvoir's concern with this conferral of meaning is how it undermines one's relationship to **moral freedom**, which she understands not as an individualistic kind of freedom but as a kind of social bond or mode of relationality in which we strive to live in ways that hold open possibilities for one another. For Beauvoir, genuine freedom is about creating the conditions for the possibility of ethical relationality, which means that moral freedom is also always political. As Beauvoir makes clear in her account of the girl's upbringing, there is an oppressive ceiling of meaning that hovers over her, limiting her horizon of possibility. In a passage that echoes *The Ethics of Ambiguity*, Beauvoir writes, "The sphere she belongs to is closed everywhere, limited ... as high as she climbs, as far as she dares to go, there will always be a ceiling over her head" (Beauvoir, 2010, p. 311). This closure is one instituted by adults through the conferral of ready-made meanings and values that deliver children into a subjectivity that forecloses their freedom. This foreclosure, however, begins with being *assigned* a particular social destiny. What Beauvoir exposes is a dominant practice in which children come into their existence through a social destiny conferred upon them – that is, they become based on what is assigned to them. Beauvoir's concern is that such conferral aims to fix the indeterminacy of becoming.

The Injustice of Becoming a Woman

There is no doubt that Beauvoir's primary concern in *The Second Sex* was to account for the injustice of becoming a woman. She exposes the ways girls and women are pressured and encouraged to desire a life in which they are second, in which they experience themselves as objects first and subjects second, in which their bodies are used and voices muted, in which their future is mutilated by femininity. Beauvoir set out to account for how such injustice became the social destiny of women. In tracking the historical, economic, social, and political conditions that create and support such injustice, Beauvoir exposes that the reality of women is neither natural nor inevitable. It is a practice, a choice that has been and continues to be made. It is a practice that is lived in ways that obscure its making, that obfuscate the reality of choice that conditions the existence of women.

On such a view – that is, in Beauvoir's view – what this means about my own becoming is that I was subjected to, and encouraged to take up, an existence that would limit my freedom. When I was assigned 'girl' at birth, I was hurled into a social destiny that would existentially, if not also physically and psychically, mutilate me. This is the injustice of becoming a girl who is supposed to become a woman. To say that my becoming a woman was a social destiny is different from saying that my life as a gendered person is a social construction. Gender was not constructed onto me as if I were a passive object. As a social destiny, my becoming was an active and passive conferral of, and embodied engagement with, meanings and expectations about who I was and should be in the world. These meanings and expectations structured my possibilities in deep ways. Without their force, without their ontological weight, I would have become differently.

That I would have become differently is indicative of another, more tacit point in Beauvoir's account of becoming in *The Second Sex*. Becoming a woman relies on being assigned such a becoming. That I was named a girl at birth was not up to me. It was not a choice I made. It was an assignment given to me by others as a result of social and historical custom. Beauvoir knew this. She knew that to become a girl who becomes a woman is a result of the intervention of others in one's life. While others are always entangled with our lives, Beauvoir's account of the injustice of becoming a woman rests on a concern about *how* and *to what extent* others intervene in who we become. What her account of becoming shows us is that 'becoming a woman' is structured by an unjust intervention. In effect, her account also opens ways to become *with others* not rooted in such injustice.

This alternative vision of becoming is one to which we will return soon. It is first necessary, however, to consider the relation between 'woman' and the body. The view of this relation as biological has long been challenged and debunked by feminist thinkers, including Beauvoir. But it is a view that has returned to the political scene as ammunition to discredit the lives of transgender women in particular, and transgender people more generally. The resurgence of this biological view is an event of patriarchy. It is disturbing and so must be redressed.

2
On Females and Women

"'People who menstruate' I'm sure there used to be a word for those people. Someone help me out," the author of the Harry Potter series tweeted on June 6, 2020, in response to an article about disparities in menstrual and health hygiene across the world. "Wumben? Wimpund? Woomud?" her tweet concluded (Rowling, 2020b). The article, "Creating a More Equal Post-COVID-19 World for People Who Menstruate," speaks about "girls, women, and non-binary persons who menstruate" during the Covid-19 pandemic who experienced intensified barriers to resources and services needed "to manage menstruation with safety, dignity, and comfort" (Sommer et al., 2020). As many others have done in a frenzy to save women from some impending non-existence when phrases like "pregnant people" or "people with uteruses" are used in discussions about reproductive health and related political issues such as contraception and abortion, these tweets take aim at the usage of "people who menstruate" in the article's title. They insist that "people" do not menstruate. That we're living in some illusory and problematic world, the kind that erases women's experience, when we use language that does not name the bodily experiences of women.

It wasn't the only tweet the author posted on June 6, 2020. Indeed, she did not hesitate to clarify her point in several other tweets: "If sex isn't real, there's no same-sex attraction. If sex isn't real, the lived reality of women globally is erased. I know and love trans people, but erasing the concept of sex removes the ability of many to meaningfully discuss their lives. It isn't hate to speak the truth" (2020c). It turns out help wasn't really needed. She already had a word in mind. A concluding tweet made this apparent: "I respect every trans person's right to live any way that feels authentic and comfortable to them. I'd march with you if you were discriminated against on the basis of being trans. At the same time, *my life has been shaped by being female.* I do not believe it's hateful to say so" (2020c; emphasis mine). The end of this tweet is important. It makes clear that the word that's gone missing is not even women, but rather *females*.

These tweets echo a sedimented "common-sense" belief that women are females, females are women. The two words are used as synonyms for a *kind* of human being, differentiated by sexual parts and reproductive capacities. To be more precise, the "common-sense" view is that 'female' names the biological sex of women. As discussed in the Introduction, gender-critical views often use the term 'natal woman' to mean a woman who is biologically female. The qualifier is really, though, unnecessary, since the gender-critical claim is that natal women are the only real women. Such a view roots existence in *being*, as opposed to becoming. One is a woman because she *is* female.

Such a position recalls Janice Raymond's *The Transsexual Empire: The Making of the She-Male* (1979), which is, as was mentioned in the Introduction, one origin of contemporary TERF discourse. In this book, Raymond affirms a metaphysical truth to bio-

On Females and Women

logical sex, to being female, that restricts the category of 'woman' to those who are biologically female. Raymond takes such a position to its most extreme, arguing that transsexual women, those who desire to and do change their bodily physiology to become women, inflict sexual violation on those who are "truly" female. "All transsexuals rape women's bodies by reducing the real female form to an artifact, appropriating this body for themselves," Raymond writes in one of the most famous and inflammatory passages in TERF history (1994, p. 104). Her claim hinges on two key points. First, there is the biological essentialist view that "real" women are biologically female. Second, there is the view that the attempt to change sex, to become female, by "biological males" is an expression of the patriarchal gesture to violate and consume women, who are and can only be "biological females." Ultimately, such a view asserts that the truth about 'woman,' what and who a woman is, is rooted in the fact of biological sex. To downplay or erase the truth of biological sex is a misogynist plot against women. Or, as Raymond says more antagonistically in the Introduction to the 1994 edition of *The Transsexual Empire*, "Transsexualism urges us to collude in the falsification of reality – that men can be real women" (1994, p. xxiii). From such a trans-exclusionary perspective, it is important to be vigilant about how the reality and experiences of those who are biologically female – that is, those who are *real* women – are erased by trans women and moves to protect and affirm trans existence in general, such as in the use of inclusive language like "people who menstruate." Without such vigilance, we'll all be guilty of self-deception, having bought into the view that biological sex doesn't determine who we are.

One way to carve out an alternative position to this trans-exclusionary one is to posit the reality of biological sex but distinguish it from, and make it non-necessary to, gender categories such as 'man' and 'woman.' Such a position is exemplified by the trans inclusive edugraphic "The Genderbread Person," which illustrates biological sex as "[t]he physical sex characteristics you're born with and develop, including genitalia, body shape, voice pitch, body hair, hormones, chromosomes, etc.," and gender identity as "[h]ow you in your head, define your gender, based on how much you align (or don't align) with what you understand to be the options for gender" (Killermann, 2018). "The Genderbread Person" also takes aim at the myth of discrete binary sex and gender, illustrating sex and gender identity as spectrums in which there are infinite possibilities. This use of the sex–gender distinction aims to be a trans inclusive gesture that affirms the reality of biological sex but does not demand that it dictate the truth of being a woman, man, or any other gender. It means that one can be female, but not a woman. It is the most common rebuttal to gender-critical and TERF views that biological sex is the essence of being a woman or a man. This mobilization of the sex–gender distinction also makes room to acknowledge that, when it comes to trans experience, transitions are not only or always about gender identity; that the reality of biological sex can and does matter as central to an individual's transition, but it is not the arbiter of truth regarding who one is as a woman, man, or other gendered person.

While this position offers an alternative to the gender-critical insistence that sex is not only real but the truth of being a woman, it still leaves a question many people want to understand: If 'woman' is not synonymous with 'female,' and if biological sex does not correlate to gender identity, how is it that most women seem to be females? To put it another way: What exactly is the relationship between 'female' and 'woman'? In the con-

On Females and Women

text of the history of feminist theorizing, this question often takes a different form: What about the truth of the (sexed) body? One popular response to these questions is the social constructionist response, which highlights how patriarchal beliefs about gender construct the very category of biological sex, making biological sex a normative and prescriptive rather than objective category. In other words, the category of biological sex and identification of someone as having a biological sex does not name, but constructs, reality.

Beauvoir responds to the matter of embodiment differently, offering a unique perspective on the relation between 'female' and 'woman.' As discussed in chapter 1, Beauvoir does not believe being a woman is a biological destiny. She argues that it is a social one. How biological essentialism is used to justify women's inferiority and subordination to men is central to her consideration of the kind of social destiny 'becoming a woman' is. For her, patriarchal ideology is rooted in the view that biological sex proves an essential difference in who men and women are. She takes views that ground women's *being* in biology to justify the mutilated existence women assume. She does not, however, claim that physiological differences do not matter at all. And, perhaps more interestingly, she does not deny that there is a relationship between 'woman' and 'female.' Yet that relationship is not at all what gender-critical and TERF views take it to be. For Beauvoir, it is true that women are female beings, but it is also not the case that being female refers to any objective truth out there in the world. Indeed, for Beauvoir, 'female' is, just like 'woman', experientially constituted. The aim of this chapter is to describe what exactly this claim means and how it can help us navigate and change the landscape of gendered embodiment in liberatory ways.

The Fact of Being Female

Contrary to what gender-critical readings like to suggest, Beauvoir does not assert that biological sex is the foundation or truth of being a woman. In fact, she thinks such a view is a *common assumption*. "Woman? Very simple, say those who like simple answers: She is a womb, an ovary, she is a female," Beauvoir states in the first lines of the "Biological Data" chapter. "[T]his word [female] is enough to define her" (2010, p. 21). While Beauvoir acknowledges that such a definition of woman exists, she doesn't buy it. She thinks it is an ideological conception of what a woman is and goes to great lengths to lay bare this reality.

In fact, she begins to expose the ideological underpinnings of this definition of woman as female in the opening lines of *The Second Sex* when she remarks on the contradictory views of so-called experts who, on the one hand, define women as females, but also proclaim that there are females who are not women. According to these experts, a woman is not just a female, but they expect that women "must take part in ... femininity" (p. 3). In addition, Beauvoir also takes the common assumption to be a flawed view of human existence. She refuses the view that our existence is fixed or determined for us in advance of how we exist in the world. Defining women as female is thus, she argues, both a matter of patriarchal ideology and a flawed philosophical understanding of what it is to be a human being.

Beauvoir therefore rejects the idea that 'female' is enough to define what a woman is. However, at the very same time, she also asserts, "And the fact is that she [woman] is a female" and asks, "what unique kind of female is realized in woman?" (p. 21). So, are women female human beings? Beauvoir's answer: yes, and not necessarily.

On Females and Women

Often, the existence of males and females is taken to be universal and natural. It is a biological fact, some might say, and therefore an obvious, indisputable truth. But, as Beauvoir points out, the division of the sexes "does not occur universally in nature" (p. 21). Although biology can attest that sexual differentiation exists, it does not show that differentiation always results in two sexed types. Grace Lavery (2023) explains this point as follows: "Beauvoir's feminism depended on a refusal of the notion that different sex *characteristics* produced differently sexed *organisms* and the conviction that, while biological *traits* could be sexed, whole people can't in any reliable or comprehensive way." While people have come to accept that there are human males and human females, as a biological fact, Beauvoir challenges, and ultimately undermines, this as an essential fact. It may be the case that there are human males and human females, but this is a contingent fact, not one that is inevitable.

Of course, however, people point to the fact of reproduction to claim that two sexes do exist. They must! Beauvoir shows, though, that reproduction takes place in several ways, including self-fertilization. Her point? Two sexes need not exist for a species to reproduce. "The phenomena of asexual multiplication and parthenogenesis are neither more or less fundamental than those of sexual reproduction," she writes (2010, p. 26). Moreover, Beauvoir points to biological data that highlights the ambiguity of sexual differentiation. "In nature," she writes, "nothing is ever completely clear: the two types, male and female, are not always sharply distinguished" (p. 38).

When sexual differentiation is a part of a species, Beauvoir is adamant that reproduction is not necessarily reliant on the typification of discrete beings into 'male' and 'female.' Rather, differentiation is a cellular matter:

there are ova and sperm. "[G]amete specification does not lead to individual specification," she writes (p. 29), and even when such specification does occur "the barriers between them are not tight ... males and females develop more as variation on a common base" (p. 29). In other words, while we can point to distinct reproductive cells, it is not possible to say these cells are so different that movement between them is not possible. They are, rather, variations on a theme. She does, of course, acknowledge that, amongst humans, reproduction often occurs along the two types of biological sex, but this sexed typification is not a mere given – it is *taken on*, meaning: assumed or lived in a concrete context. For her, it's not that there aren't physiological or reproductive differences at the biological level through which reproduction occurs. Her point is that the emergence of 'male' and 'female' are typifications that occur in a total context, not in brute nature. As Lavery (2023) explains, "So, according to Beauvoir, sex is differentiable at the scale of the cell, but since there exist organisms in which sex cells of both sexes are found, we therefore cannot use the fact of sexual dimorphism as a basis for the sexual classification of individuals or groups."

We can begin to think about what it means for 'male' and 'female' to be taken on by understanding how Beauvoir understands *facts*. As mentioned in the previous chapter, Beauvoir claims there are two dimensions to human existence: facticity and transcendence. **Facticity** refers to the givens of being, or that which just is. The factical dimensions of our lives are undeniable, but not definitive. For instance, there is no escaping the fact that we are mortal, that we will die. At the same time, how we live our mortality, including how we die, how long we live, what the total conditions of our mortality are, exceeds facticity because human existence is also transcendence. She understands **transcendence** to be the meaning-making and world-building dimension of our lives. It is what we do and create, which is shaped by and anchored in facticity, but not determined by it. In *The Second Sex*, Beauvoir describes the factical dimension of our lives in terms of **immanence** – the life-sustaining, passive and cyclical aspects of being human – whereas transcendence is future-oriented, world-building activity related to the movement of freedom. For Beauvoir, human existence is always both immanence and transcendence, rooted in undeniable facts that we cannot evade, and yet we're not wholly constrained to those facts. So, while there are inevitable facts at play in our experience, how we experience these facts, how they come to have meaning, and how we negotiate them, are matters of our transcendent activity. Regarding physiological facts in particular, Beauvoir's view is that they are undeniable. We cannot deny, she claims, the fact of our bodies and the fact that bodily differences exist. Reproductive physiological differences exist. Penises. Vulvas. Sperm. Ova. Testosterone. Estrogen. Obviously, these "parts" are facts of human life. But she argues that the significance of 'female' can only be understood "in its concrete reality" – that is, in the entanglement of facticity and transcendence (Beauvoir, 2010, p. 26). These dimensions of our lives are inseparable.

What Beauvoir wants us to reconsider is the role of such facts in human existence. For her, the fact of being male or female is "a fact that has neither ontological nor empirical basis" and its "impact cannot a priori be understood" (p. 26). In other words, biological sex is not the essence or ground of our existence, nor is its significance legible prior to our experience of it. So, she believes that "[t]he differentiation of individuals into males and females" does exist, but she insists it "occurs as an irreducible and contingent fact" (p. 23). In effect, 'female' does not name a natural phenomenon. Rather, as philosopher Jennifer McWeeny (2023) shows in her reading of Beauvoir, being female is an experiential phenomenon. For Beauvoir, 'female' bears no meaning beyond the context in which being female is experienced. She puts this most clearly when she writes, "In truth these facts [of human physiology] cannot be denied: but they do not carry their meaning in themselves. As soon as we accept a human perspective, defining the body starting from existence, biology becomes an abstract science" (Beauvoir, 2010, p. 46). Accordingly, the concept of female does not refer to a purely anatomical or physiological truth. It describes a particular way in which human beings become individuated. And Beauvoir is clear: that particular way of becoming individuated has everything to do with keeping women in a subordinated position. The individuation is not, then, natural; it is, for her, a political maneuver of patriarchy.

This is going to be a difficult perspective for some to understand or even agree with because it flies in the face of the dominant way of thinking about biological sex. It's important to note, though, that Beauvoir's claim that 'female' is experiential, not natural, does not mean that physiological differences are not a factual truth of our lives. I have no doubt about my body, especially because others have constantly reminded me of my body throughout my life – sometimes in terrible ways, other times in the most pleasurable of ways. Beauvoir has no doubt about this either. She does not believe the body itself is socially constructed. She does, however, refuse to reduce human existence to our physiology or biology. She is nowhere clearer about this than when she writes, "man is not a natural species: he is a historical idea" (p. 45). She reiterates this point in the "Conclusion" of *The Second Sex*: "in spite of legends, no physiological destiny imposes eternal hostility on the Male and Female as such ... humanity is something other than a [biological] species: it is a historical becoming; it is defined by the way it assumes natural facticity" (p. 753). Notice here she does not say that we are defined or determined by natural facticity. Rather, we are defined by how we *assume* our facticity – that is, by how we live as physiological beings, embody ourselves, our bodies, in the concrete circumstances we live in. In other words, "individuals are never left to their natures" (p. 47).

The view that humans are not a natural or biological species speaks to Beauvoir's view, shared by other thinkers who draw on **phenomenology**. For a phenomenologist like Beauvoir, the body is not something we have; *the body is not a thing*. Rather, one's body is central to one's **situation,** or the total, concrete context in which someone assumes who they are. By this, Beauvoir means that one's body is one's grasp and hold on the world. My body is how I have a world, but it is not definitive of my world. There is, Beauvoir posits, an experiential and generative relationship between the body and the world. The world, the context in which one lives, is mediated and shaped by one's bodily experience, and vice versa. This means that we cannot reduce our bodies or ourselves to physiological parts, but we also cannot neglect them either. As central to our situation, the fact of physiological difference does shape who we become, but how and to what extent it shapes who we become is bound up with the world in which we experience our bodies.

What does all this mean about the relation between 'female' and 'woman', or between 'woman' and *being female*? Beauvoir does, in fact, assert that to be a woman is to be a female, but *not* as a natural fact. A 'woman' *is* a female being, but this is a historical matter just as much as a physiological one. Since we are not a natural species, it is impossible to say that a woman is naturally female. That women are female is a matter of circumstance. Women, therefore, are female beings, but female does not point to any brute biological reality. When it comes to human existence, the fact of being 'female' is contingent. As the concrete conditions of our lives change, so too will our understanding and experience of facticity. It is no wonder, then, that working to maintain concrete conditions as they have been, to *legislate* that biological sex is a truth to being a woman, is central to the elimination of trans possibilities, for trans possibilities offer us new ways to assume our bodies, to take on our facticity. These possibilities threaten the common assumption that Beauvoir herself exposes as a contingent fact, not an inevitable truth.

There's an important scene in trans activist and author Leslie Feinberg's groundbreaking novel *Stone Butch Blues* (2014) that sheds light on the concrete implications of Beauvoir's understanding of 'female' and the relation between being female and being a woman. In the novel, the main character, Jess, is a gender-nonconforming, masculine-presenting person. Jess is regularly referred to as "sir," as most people believe, based on perception, that Jess is a non-trans man. In one scene in the novel, Jess realizes they have a vaginal infection that needs treatment. Reluctantly, Jess goes to a women's health clinic in their neighborhood. When they arrive at the clinic, the receptionist smiles at Jess and says, "This clinic is for women" (Feinberg, 2014, p. 257). Jess nods and whispers in reply, "I know. I have a vaginal infection." The receptionist, baffled that someone like Jess could have a vaginal infection, tells Jess, "Have a seat, sir." While Jess waits amidst a room full of stares, a clinic employee named Roz scolds Jess for taking up space at a women's clinic. "You may think you're a woman," Roz tells Jess, "but that doesn't mean you are one." Full of rage and discomfort, Jess gets up, ready to bolt from the clinic. They didn't go there in

On Females and Women

the first place claiming to be a woman – in fact, Jess was hesitant to go because it was a *women's* clinic. But where else was Jess to go? The clinic's doctor blocks Jess from leaving and, without denying Jess's reality or being suspicious of Jess's presence at the clinic, the doctor takes Jess seriously, giving Jess a prescription and the medical advice they need. On the way out, wanting to remember the doctor, Jess asks Roz for the doctor's name. But Roz, still annoyed with Jess's presence, rudely says, "You got what you wanted, now leave" (p. 259). "You're wrong, Roz," Jess replies; "I got what I needed. You have no idea how much I want."

Jess's experience is instructive. On the one hand, it highlights the experiential dimension of 'female' as it is bound to 'woman.' Jess is not and does not appear to others to be a woman. Jess is also not taken to be a female human being, or even treated as a human being for that matter. Even if, as Beauvoir suggests at the beginning of *The Second Sex*, some human females are not taken to be women because they are not feminine, it's not necessarily true that they are female either and that is because, as Beauvoir shows in the "Biological Data" chapter, being female *is* experiential, meaning it is related to the entire context in which that experience takes place. Jess's experience at the women's clinic speaks to this point very clearly. Jess does not arrive at the clinic because they are female; they go to the clinic because of the specific situation they face. A women's clinic is *the* only option Jess has. And yet, at the clinic, Jess is also not necessarily understood to be female. The doctor certainly treats Jess's bodily facticity and does not treat Jess as a woman. But it's not necessarily clear that the doctor believes Jess is female either. The doctor just treats Jess and gives Jess what they need for their infection. Who Jess is is not the main issue at stake; it's whether or not Jess is treated with respect and dignity.

So, while Roz is a total jerk for her insistence that Jess is not deserving of care, her refusal to recognize Jess as female and a woman could have been affirmative had it not been predicated on excluding Jess from a needed material resource.

Interestingly, in contrast to Roz's disgust with and rejection of Jess as a woman, and against the doctor's treatment of Jess as a person who has a uterus but is not female, gender-critical perspectives today are likely to say that Jess should be served by the women's clinic because clearly "she" is a female human being and has the genitalia to prove it. Most gender-critical views can't exclude trans masculine individuals from the category of 'biological female,' which means they are really, truly, no matter what, always women masquerading as men. So, in today's context where biological essentialism is routinely mobilized, the insistence that someone like Jess is female means that Jess is also a woman and this will always override a trans person's self-definition. Importantly, even if Jess recognizes the contingent fact of their body, their self-definition may not only be about not being a woman, but it may also be about not being female. In other words, it's possible to affirm that Jess is neither a woman nor a female and still acknowledge the facticity of the body. Moreover, given that 'female' is experiential, it's also possible to affirm that trans women are not only women, but also female, regardless of one's genital status. It's possible that our bodies are variable, variations, and rich with possibilities. Yet, given how dominant views so tightly restrict our capacity to think and live, it's no surprise that the common assumption Beauvoir identifies persists. But what if we all took a note from Jess and acknowledged the fact of our bodies and allowed for other possibilities for ourselves? What if we all took our cue from the doctor and offered people what they need without ridiculing how they want to take on and live their facticity? Beauvoir's conception of 'female' as experiential, rather than biologically determinative, certainly opens space for such possibilities.

Let's Talk about "Sex"

In 1969, American trans activist Virginia Prince began to use the word 'transgenderal' to refer to her own experience of being trans. In contrast to the medical use of 'transgenderism' at the time, Prince made a distinction between people who undergo surgeries as central to their transition and people, like herself, who do not. Prince's work as a writer and activist helped push forward the now popular, widely used distinction between transsexual and transgender. The term **transsexual** typically refers to a person whose gender does not align with an assignment of and expectations around sexed embodiment and who has undergone medical reassignment to alter their bodies, while the term **transgender** typically refers to a person whose gender has moved away from an unchosen, nonconsensual starting place, but who does not necessarily undergo medical reassignment. By the 1990s, transgender, and trans for short, had become an "umbrella term" meant to describe a variety of ways of being trans, including being transsexual. The upshot of the umbrella term was that it recognizes that trans experience is not a monolith. One of its limits, however, is that, as trans scholar Paisley Currah points out, "placing so many different ways of failing to conform to gender norms under a conceptually smooth category of transgender gets in the way of identifying specific forms of exclusion that affect people under the 'umbrella' differently" (2022, p. xiii). Today, 'transsexual' is often taken to be an outdated, pejorative term, due to how medical "experts" pathologized the term and the people they applied it to. As a result, non-trans people are told not to use the term 'transsexual,' and if they do use it, to make sure the person they are calling transsexual has given permission for the term's use. In contexts rife with trans antagonisms, I don't disagree with such suggestions. But it's also important to recognize that there are transsexual people who still embrace the term, and, in doing so, draw attention to how the experiential dimension of natural facticity *does* matter. In other words, while some people like Prince don't want, don't choose to, or can't alter their physiology, some people want and need to alter it. Experientially, trans existence is not, then, all about gender. Trans experience can be about sex – if, by that, we mean physiological differences.

The intention here is not to subject or expose trans people to further scrutiny. The bodily privacy of trans people is routinely denied, and non-trans people have been and continue to be overly curious about the genital status of trans people. Both moves to "know" trans people turn them into what philosopher Amy Marvin (2020) calls "curios," or objects of fascination, whereby their lived experience is annihilated for the sake and interest of the non-trans onlooker's curiosity. This problematic, objectifying kind of curiosity turns trans people into mere bodies, and thus into things. In *Curiosity and Power* (2021), Perry Zurn argues that there is another kind of curiosity, a trans curiosity, that can operate as a mode of resistance to objectifying curiosity. As Zurn puts it, "Curiosity is not only present in trans people's accounts of their own experiences with others, however; it also functions as a tool of resistance by which trans people foster rich personal and social life typically denied them by institutionalized manifestations of curiosity, especially the spectacle-erasure formation" (p. 185). This world-building, trans-affirming curiosity is the kind of curiosity needed in the face of trans antagonisms that seek to erode bodily autonomy, including bans on gender-affirming care and banning trans girls and women from sports. We can be curious about how and when so-called sex differences matter and why there is still a need to talk about "sex."

The significance of such physiology is also one Beauvoir's view does not deny. The fact that our bodies do not determine who we are does not mean that who we are is not at all bound up with our own bodily experience in and of the world, in relation to others, and in relation to our desires and needs. Even if our bodies are not determinative of who we are, insofar as our bodies are our situation in and of the world, the facts of our bodies do matter. It's really no wonder, then, why so many of us, trans and non-trans alike, alter, modify, and change our bodies as a condition of becoming who we are. Transsexual experience is just a variation on this theme. That some forms of bodily modification are taken to be *more* significant than others is what Beauvoir would call contingent, a reality that hinges on the values and conventions of particular, concrete circumstance.

In *Sex Is as Sex Does* (2022), Currah argues that we need to consider sex as a matter of governance, rather than as a matter of the nature of our being. As Currah shows, sex as a mode of classification is a central way states make distinctions among people to govern them. That states are invested in 'sex' – which is to say that sex classification matters politically – is neither an innocent nor natural phenomenon; a state's investment in sex classification – who is *really* an M or F, or whether people can be X – is about how a state and actors, such as politicians and lobbyists who work to secure the state's interests, exert power over individuals. Currah puts it this way:

> the only thing we can say for sure about what sex means is what a particular state actor says it means. Unlike the definitions put forth by individuals or circulated by activists and researchers, state declarations of sex are backed by the force of the law ... sex is not a thing, a property, or a trait, but the outcome of decisions backed by legal authority. (2002, p. 39)

Currah's point is not meant to deny facticity, as Beauvoir might say. Rather, Currah's point is that talking about sex must take into consideration *that* and *how* sex matters is up to the state.

In the context of the United States, Currah exposes how the state changes the meaning of sex to fit its interests, not to uphold any biological truth. It is rather about "what sex *does* for a particular state project," now and in the past (p. 143). Indeed, Currah shows that sex classification only matters to the state today when it is needed to uphold a particular social order, one rooted in trans exclusion. So, far from a biological truth, sex itself is a legal and political classification, and it is a system of classification rife with inconsistencies and contradictions. The result is that in some contexts the state allows rather easily for sex reclassification, while in other contexts sex classification is stubborn. Take, for instance, the reality that in many places in the United States (and elsewhere) it is easy to change one's sex classification on an identification document like a driver's license. When I changed the F to an X on my driver's license, all I needed to do was go to the Department of Motor Vehicles and fill out paperwork. The sex reclassification happened because I requested that it did. I didn't need a medical expert to authorize this change. I didn't need to prove anything. But, to use another example from Currah, if I were to be arrested and sent to county jail, the sex classification on my driver's license, the one based on my self-definition, would not be backed by the force of the law. I would be free to think of myself as X, but the law would still think of me as F. Although the state would be making a contradiction, what is important is that, in a given context, sex classification means what the state wants it to mean. The ease of identificatory reclassifications also goes against bathroom bills that seek to regulate who uses what bathroom on the basis of sex, and trans athlete bans at youth and professional levels that bar trans people from playing or competing in sports based on their self-definition. So, even despite some state moves to disinvest from sex classification, the state still heavily invests in binary sex classifications. As Currah shows, this investment not only is the persistence of a conservative gender order, but also "causes real harm" (p. 151).

Currah talks about sex because trans studies and trans politics moved away from sex talk to gender talk. The transgender paradigm, as it overrode transsexual, shifting attention away from sex to gender, leaves little room to address what sex is really doing in politics. If regulating sex classification is what the state does to maintain a particular social order, it means considerations of the meaning of sex are inseparable from the realm of the political. It also means that political struggles are struggles about our bodies and who gets to control the meaning of our bodies, of ourselves. It's important, then, to not deny that sex matters; it's important to talk about sex, but we must take care with how we talk about sex, with how we understand what it means, and how we, individually and collectively, come to assume our facticity.

The gender-critical and trans-antagonistic rejection of the claim "trans women are women" is rooted in the assumption that 'woman' is synonymous with biological sex. This view is, however, just one kind of sex talk. It has a use, which, as both Currah and Beauvoir show, is to regulate and limit existence – that is, how and who we get to become – by regulating and defining the significance of our bodies. This use is bound up with various histories of power that seek to harm some, while protecting the values, meanings, and material gains of the most privileged, including the most privileged of women.

On (and Away from) Sexed and Gendered Categorization

For those of us who inhabit social, political, and educational spaces aiming to be inclusive of trans people and trans possibilities, there is almost always attention given to the language used to describe people. The aim of such attention is to be trans inclusive, insofar as linguistic categorization on the basis of sex and gender have the potential to exclude, as they historically have, trans people. To right such a wrong, an event that wants to be welcoming and inclusive of all women might say, "This event welcomes all women, including cis and trans women." Or an event for men historically reserved for and occupied by non-trans men might say, "We welcome all men and male-identified people." Or "women-identified folks" and "male-identified folks" might be used instead of the terms 'women' and 'men.' Insofar as language is a key way to build sociality and relationality, this struggle over what language to use is important. Moreover, if we take seriously that linguistic classifications do matter in terms of how we assume or experience our bodies, then the language we use to refer to, to name, to give meaning to our bodies–selves, and to others, is without a doubt significant.

Given the always evolving, shifting terrain of sexed and gendered language, it is not clear there's an obvious prescription. That would be too easy. Besides, if there's anything this chapter has tried to show, it's that there are *many* possibilities, and likely should be, for how we describe, define, and name our facticity. It does, however, seem evident that language that upholds assumptions about our gendered/sexed existence as biological is problematic. If 'female' and 'woman' operate synonymously, then perhaps using 'female' to mean women (or 'male' to mean men) isn't necessarily problematic, though likely unnecessary, so long as 'female' is inclusive of trans women and 'male' is inclusive of trans men. But if, by 'female', one means women and non-binary people who are "biologically female," then we're likely playing on the turf of trans-exclusionary sex classifications.

The current reality of sport does, of course, rely on regulated sex classifications that, for many, seem to be evident biological categories. This form of segregation is typically justified by an appeal to two mutually exclusive sex categories in which one category has a clear, natural advantage over the other. In such a context, trans athletes are always framed as the problem. Rather than considering whether a sports system that does not, and often refuses to, accommodate and include trans people is just in the first place, trans athletes become the ones who are to be banned from sport. With the focus on trans athletes, rather than on the structuring of sport itself, it is trans people who have to make deliberate decisions about the extent to which they will medically transition, as is often the case for non-binary and trans masc people and trans men who compete in "women's sports," or they will have their medical transition subjected to deep scrutiny, as is often the case for trans women who compete in "women's sports." Although such regulation is done in the name of fairness, it's unclear whether trans athletes have a disproportionate unfair physiological advantage over non-trans athletes. In the absence of such knowledge, the rules, policies, and practices that do exist to regulate physiological differences favor non-trans athletes, especially non-trans women.

Yet, as numerous scholars, advocates, and activists for inclusion in sport have pointed out, the focus on non-trans women is a matter of excluding any body that does not fit the ideal of 'female.' The result is that Black non-trans women are just as likely to have their bodies scrutinized and even banned from sport because of failing to fit the norm of 'female' even if they are not trans. This kind of racialized regulation of the categories 'woman' and 'female' is precisely what has happened, and continues to happen, to South African runner Caster Semenya. Moreover, even if trans athletes could have some physiological advantage, it's also the case that non-trans athletes can and do have physiological advantages relative to trans athletes. Bodies come in all sizes, shapes, and capacities for strength and fitness that are not at all rooted in a non-trans/trans distinction. It is thus the case that sex categorizations in sport are said to be about pure biological categories, but in fact they are not. This is not to say that all sports that are currently segregated must be desegregated, but rather that the current logic of justification is not natural: it is a matter of regulation. If there is to exist "women's sports" and "men's sports," then it's important to consider how to employ such categorizations in non-exclusionary ways.

Perhaps, then, what matters most is that we focus not simply on getting the language right, but on making sure material resources are distributed in ways that do not harm the most vulnerable of people. For instance, if bathrooms are sex-segregated and there's a concern about exclusion (which there should be), the first question shouldn't be: "What's the right word or phrase to use for this bathroom?" It should be "Who needs to use this restroom?" and "How can space be restructured to make that use possible?" Or, for an event planned for "women's health," the questions that should be asked are: "What work is 'women' doing in the event more generally?" "Who may need the information distributed at this event, but who would likely feel excluded by the title?" By focusing on how we use categorizations and what their effects are we may be better equipped to secure life chances for trans people.

Ultimately, if we take seriously that physiological differences are experiential, and so only lived and defined within a context, it is impossible to ignore that how some physiological differences come to matter and come to shape who we get to become, and how we become, is a political matter, not a biological one. This is a point Beauvoir makes. To accept that the truth of our lives does not reside in our biological sex exposes us to the reality that the social destiny of "becoming a woman" is up to us. If we are not, as Beauvoir claims, a natural species, how we proceed with and respond to ideological forces that work to turn our becoming into being is up to us. This leaves us with an important question: how ought we to become? This question is the focus of the next chapter.

3
An Ethics of Trans Affirmation

In April 2021, the headquarters of the Madrid Lesbian, Gay, Bisexual, and Transsexual Collective (COGAM), located in the city's queer neighborhood, Chueca, were vandalized, covered with graffiti of transphobic slurs. Among them were some of the common taglines of anti-trans discourse, including "sex 'doesn't equal' gender" and "reproductive exploiters." Just a few months later in August 2021, one of Madrid's LGBT bookstores, Mary Read, was also vandalized with anti-trans graffiti. The storefront, spray-painted with sayings like "No to the hormonation of under-aged children" and "Saying the truth is not a crime" tainted the queer and trans-affirming space (Bretín, 2021). In the same month, across the Atlantic in Ottawa, Canada, trans-affirmative posters were put up across the city by the Ottawa Coalition to End Violence Against Women (McArdle, 2021). The posters were vandalized in various ways with anti-trans messaging, and met with a counter campaign of trans-exclusionary stickers, some of which read: "Woman is not a costume," "Gender is not another word for sex," and "Gender is Fleeting, Sex is Forever." Months earlier, in February 2021, just south of the Canadian border, Marjorie Taylor Greene, an American far-right politician who serves in the US House of Representatives posted an anti-trans sign outside her office door that read: "There are TWO genders: Male & Female. 'Trust The Science!'" (Duster, 2021). Across the hall from Greene was the office of Marie Newman, a state representative from Illinois whose daughter is transgender.

These discrete anti-trans gestures around the world can be read as responses to legislative efforts that sought to affirm transgender people. For instance, in June 2021, after months of pushing for its acceptance, the Spanish government approved a draft of a gender recognition bill, allowing anyone over the age of 14 to change their gender legally, as it is marked on issued identification cards, without a medical diagnosis or hormone therapy. In 2023, a different version of the bill became law, increasing the age from 14 to 16. At the time of Greene's antagonistic poster hanging, the Equality Act, which would amend Title VI of the US Civil Rights Act of 1964 to ban discrimination on the basis of a person's self-determined gender identity, was under review. Greene was attempting to block the Equality Act, claiming it destroys women's rights. Although the bill passed the US House of Representatives, it failed to move through the US Senate. These forms of legislation are not necessarily a boon for trans people. Trans scholars like Dean Spade (2011) have made clear that the legal recognition of trans people can be understood as another way for states to administer – that is, regulate – individual experience and collective arrangements of gender. In other words, getting the state to see you for who you really are isn't necessarily liberatory; it's a means of being governed. Regardless, though, it's clear these legislative moves to recognize trans existence instigate ire on the streets. The numerous instances of anti-trans vandalism exemplify trans-exclusionary political discourse that not only aims to delegitimize transgender people, but also refuses, rather forcefully, efforts that seek to affirm the lives of trans people.

To understand the harm of this refusal requires an address of the ethical significance of gender affirmation. In other words, we can best grasp what is wrong with the refusal to accept trans people on their terms when we know something about the significance of avowing trans experience. In mainstream discourse, gender affirmation usually means the acceptance and support of an individual's gender identity. Whether people are conscious of it or not, this conception is most often rooted in the psychological conception of gender identity, that is, the idea that gender is an internal sense an individual has of who they are as a gendered person. On the gender identity model, gender is held in distinction from biological sex, which need not but often does bear correspondence, and affirming gender identity is a matter of affirming an individual's inner, felt sense of gender, not holding an individual to a direct correspondence between biological sex and gender identity.

The psychological model of affirmation is at the heart of the most popular discourse of gender affirmation, gender-affirming care, which also serves as the basis for legislative efforts to secure the legal recognition of **self-defined gender**. In many ways, this model has proven productive. It has been a formal gateway for gender transition. Once authorities on physical and mental health began to vocalize support for gender transition, the contours of and access to care changed in ways that gave some trans people increased access. That formal gateway, and the authority of doctors in particular, has legitimized trans needs, bodies, and desires, which in turn has bolstered affirmative legislative moves.

Yet this model of gender affirmation has its limits. Most importantly, as will be discussed in the next sec-

An Ethics of Trans Affirmation

tion, gender identity discourse is not a godsend for liberatory experiences of gender. Indeed, gender identity discourse reifies dominant beliefs about and ways of knowing gender. The result is that the psychological or medical model of gender affirmation winds up securing an authoritative conception of gender, even if it also confers recognition to some trans people. The result, then, is a contradictory practice of gender affirmation. Trans people may gain recognition, but that recognition entrenches the dominant pedagogy and practice of gender. This chapter offers an alternative conception of gender affirmation, one rooted not in a psychological theory about gender, but in an ethics. To be more specific, we need a conception of gender affirmation that is about how we should relate to one another.

The relation between oneself and others was a primary concern for Beauvoir. It is possible to read this concern as at the heart of *The Second Sex*. How ought women and men to relate to one another if not through patriarchal conventions? How ought we to experience our own becoming if not mediated by patriarchal ideology? And, since others are inevitably with us in the world, how ought we to pursue our becoming collectively – that is, in relation? These are the questions that animate this chapter. While people may currently speak about gender affirmation as a matter of authorizing someone's gender identity, such a view doesn't actually get at what a world that genuinely affirms trans people requires: a particular kind of relationality. An ethics of gender affirmation helps account for why even those of us who are critical of gender identity discourse nonetheless affirm trans people's self-defined genders, full stop – and why everyone else ought to do the same.

Gender-Affirming Care Saves Lives

Gender-affirming care designates a wide range of social, psychological, and medical interventions that support an individual's gender identity when it is incongruent with their gender designated at birth. It is a model of care that rests on the standards established by the World Professional Association for Transgender Health (WPATH), which was founded in 1979. WPATH is an organization of social, physical, and mental health professionals and is the longest-standing, recognized collective authority for evidence-based care for transgender people. WPATH was originally named the Harry Benjamin International Gender Dysphoria Association (HBIGDA) after Harry Benjamin, a German American physician known for developing early practices of professional medical interventions for transsexual people. For Benjamin, such interventions were medically necessary on the basis that the dominant psychological approach to treating people with "gender identity disorder" (GID) did not cure the disorder. According to Benjamin, what was needed were medical standards that allowed people to change their sex to "fit" or "align" their body with their mind. With a nominal transition of its own in 2007, HBIGDA became WPATH, and in 2011 it issued its seventh iteration of the standards of care. This version sought to finally address the decades of criticism from trans people that WPATH's model relied on medical **gatekeeping** – the efforts to control and limit access to transition-related care and services – and the pathologization of trans experience. Rather than treating trans experience as an illness, the 2011 standards of care moved toward an affirmative model. In a statement released just prior to the new standards of care, WPATH declared, "the expression of gender characteristics, including identities, that are not stereotypically associated with one's assigned sex at birth is a common and culturally diverse human phenomenon [that] should not be judged as inherently pathological or negative" (WPATH, 2011, p. 4)

WPATH is one of the main architects and proponents of increasing access to gender-affirming care across the world. The adoption of WPATH standards by medical practitioners has no doubt led to an increase in trans people of all ages accessing the established age-appropriate medical interventions. With puberty blockers, hormone replacement therapy, and certain surgeries as viable and medically validated options, the social landscape of sex and gender is also undergoing a transition. We are not just stuck with the bodies we have. Of course, such a reality isn't new. Non-trans women have long accessed breast augmentation surgery to affirm their womanhood. Non-trans men dope themselves up with testosterone and indulge in Viagra to secure their manhood. What matters is extending such a reality to trans people. People ought to have the right to choose what feels right for them and pursue how they desire to assume their bodily existence. Although, as I discuss shortly, gender-affirming care as a model of affirmation has its limits, it does advocate for such a right, which undermines the dominant ideology about the meaning of our bodies.

It's no wonder, then, that a significant portion of anti-trans legislation and policy works to eliminate access to gender-affirming care. Most legislation targets the possibilities of trans childhoods, insisting that gender-affirming care in minors is fraught with danger. Regardless of what medical professionals say, legislation that targets gender-affirming care, legislation written by politicians and their supporters, insists that medical care that allows children to be trans is problematic. For instance, in the United States in 2023, almost half of the state legislatures had advanced bills to end gender-affirming care, especially for minors. In the state of Texas, gender-affirming care for minors has been framed as child abuse, while other states have taken a more "moderate" view, deeming it medically unsound. As of late 2023, 5 American states consider it a felony to provide gender-affirming care to minors, while 14 others have passed various sanctions and restrictions on it, all while the American Medical Association stands in opposition to the bans. Equally concerning, the National Health Service (NHS) in England ended its reliance on the gender-affirming care model for minors, moving away from WPATH standards and promoting instead a view that minors need only psychoeducation and psychotherapy. These new NHS guidelines also strongly discourage socially affirmative transition practices for minors, such as the use of chosen names and pronouns. These political efforts to "save and protect" children are neither innocent nor benevolent. A moral panic like this is about generating widespread concern over an alleged threat for the sake of shoring up dominant ideologies and relations of power. Take, for instance, moral panics over comics and books written by American author Judy Blume. Such panics targeted the "deviant" or "subversive" content, including representations of crime, infidelity, sex, pregnancy, or menstruation. If such content is to be feared, it's not because it is dangerous per se. Rather, such content violates social and cultural norms, offering children access to knowledge and ideas that would change their understanding of the world, and, possibly, even themselves. Teenagers may, for instance, come to understand and live sexual activity as pleasurable rather than as only a part of reproduction. Effort to prevent children from accessing such content is thus a way to maintain the status quo. Even if adults had genuine concern for children in such a moral panic, their fears were wrong. Their fears were not about children, but about control.

In response to the emergent legislative zeitgeist against gender-affirming care in the United States, WPATH released a statement of opposition on March 8, 2023. In it WPATH's president, Dr. Marci Bowers, insists, "Anti-transgender health care legislation is not about protections for children but about eliminating transgender persons on a micro and macro scale" (WPATH, 2023). Echoing that gender-affirming care is a matter of life and death, the president of USPATH, the United States affiliate of WPATH, Dr. Maddie Deutsch, urges that "Medical professionals and experts who research and practice in this field must be able to do their jobs in providing life-saving care for their patients without legislative intervention" (WPATH, 2023).

Trans scholars and advocates, as well as trans people more generally, have voiced criticism about WPATH for its gatekeeping and, until more recently, its pathologization of trans experience. Neither are unique to WPATH. Gatekeeping by medical and psychiatric doctors is a salient feature of trans experience. Although some doctors may be willing to allow for gender-affirming care, it is not up to a trans person whether they can receive such care. Rather, the gender-affirming care model rests on a model of authority in which the doctor is positioned as the final arbiter over trans possibilities. Contrast this reality to procedures such as breast augmentation for non-trans women, which are taken, by the Western medical world, to be *elective* and not pathological. Even as the standards of care set forth by WPATH move in directions that minimize transness as pathological, the power of doctors to authorize care remains. Bringing trans experience in proximity to the medical establishment does not finally allow people to be trans – they already are. Rather, this proximity opens a complicated web of agency and constraint, of possibility and limitation, of access and restriction.

Underlying the standards of care, and in turn the reality of gatekeeping, is the history of **gender identity theory**, which distinguishes between biological sex and gender and proposses that gender identity is an internal, psychological phenomenon. This theory is often targeted by gender-critical feminists as not only erroneous, but, in the words of Kathleen Stock, "intellectually confused and concretely harmful" (2021, p. 40). They might be shocked to know that trans scholars also have serious critiques of and concerns about gender identity theory. The concept of gender, and subsequent iterations of it as 'gender role' and 'gender identity,' was a medical invention, largely established by psychologist John Money, and then leveraged by Money and his colleague Robert Stoller, in their work with intersex children and later trans patients at Johns Hopkins throughout the 1940s, 1950s, and 1960s. For Money, gender indicated a dimension of embodiment distinct from biological sex. While biological sex was commonly viewed to be both a simplistic biological category and an existentially determinative one, Money found himself amid research and human experience that suggested otherwise. As Jules Gill-Peterson explains in *Histories of the Transgender Child* (2018), Money was at the heart of an epistemological crisis over the category of sex. It had "become an unwieldy biological category" composed over various features, "none of them exerting what amounted to a deterministic influence" (p. 97). Money's intervention in the crisis was to fashion a new category that could keep the dominant binary view of sexed embodiment intact. In his research on intersex children, Money proposed that gender roles were learned and could therefore stabilize "ambiguous" and indeterminate sex. Money established a protocol to assign gender to intersex children for the sake of "normal" social development. In the 1950s, Money undertook research with psychologists Joan and John Hampson that ultimately insisted on the necessity of medical intervention to align the sexed body with gender. They argued that "a gender role that contradicted the visible body could be identified as pathological *because it might lead to social stigma or psychological distress*" (Gill-Peterson, 2018, p. 117).

This position became the justification for "coercive and normalizing intervention into intersex children's bodies" (pp. 98–9). It also became the foundation of American trans medicine. The medical insistence that the visible body should align with gender sanctioned medical interventions for trans embodiment. Sex reassignment was cast as the completion of "normal" development and framed any incongruence between one's body and one's sense of self as pathological. Far from a liberatory medical technology, the medical invention of gender and the gender identity theory was actually a normalizing device. It was not rooted in trans affirmation. "[T]he concept of gender greatly reinforced the binary coherence of sex" and established "a vicious clinical force that disqualified less medicalized or nonmedicalized forms of trans and intersex life" (Gill-Peterson, 2018, pp. 126–7).

In the context of contemporary gender-affirming care, gender identity theory is central to access to and approval of care. In order to receive care, a trans person's experience must fit the demands of the medically established discourse. In a critical analysis of his pursuit of a double mastectomy for top surgery, trans legal scholar Dean Spade describes how his experience was governed by the psychological conception of gender identity and the related diagnosis and "treatment" of GID. In "Mutilating Gender," Spade (2013) describes how his access to gender-affirming care was dependent on whether his experience fit the expectations and assumptions of the medical model, especially that of "transsexual childhood narrative." Spade is regularly asked to speak to "when he first knew" – that is, to describe his gender identity as emergent in childhood. Having a childhood narrative has long been a necessary condition for access to gender-affirming medical care. That is, a trans person *must have* a childhood narrative or else they will be denied care. From the medical perspective, the childhood indication of an internal gender identity speaks to a transgression that must be corrected not for the patient's autonomy, but to end their pathology and allow them to live a normal life. Spade puts it this way: "In order to get authorization for body alteration, this childhood must be produced, and the GID diagnosis accepted, maintaining an idea of two discrete gender categories that normally contain everyone but occasionally are wrongly assigned, requiring correction to reestablish the norm" (2013, p. 321).

The "transsexual childhood narrative," although seemingly objective because it comes from medicine, and affirmative because it affords access to care, enforces a certain reality of trans experience, one that relies on the conception of 'gender' established by Money and his colleagues. The expectation is that all people have a gender identity, which is an acute reality for trans people who cannot live theirs out. As a basis for gender-affirming care, the theory of gender identity is seemingly unproblematic. But the theory requires trans people to speak in its terms regardless of whether that is their personal experience. Some of us, for instance, do not have a childhood narrative, but nevertheless do not experience ourselves in accordance with our birth assignment. Some of us do have a childhood narrative, but don't experience it as dysphoric or as a maladjustment that must be corrected (Awkward-Rich, 2022). Some of us

An Ethics of Trans Affirmation

don't care to be "normal," but *desire* certain medical interventions (Chu, 2018). So, although the frame of 'gender identity' may seem all well and good if it creates access to care, it is nevertheless authoritative and normalizing. There is a demand to speak in its terms. It is not therefore an objective reality to be discovered about each of us; it is imposed on us.

The expectations and assumptions of the theory of gender identity do not just frame access to medical care. They also infiltrate everyday social practices, even ones that aim to be trans-affirming. It is often the case that non-trans people expect that being trans is a condition that begins in childhood. If it does begin in childhood, the assumption is that it is something to be treated. There is also the assumption that someone's experience of gender is a matter of an internal identity such that affirmation is an affirmation of a person's essence. When, for instance, asking for pronouns, my wager is that most people think they are finding out some inner truth about a person. Such is the sedimentation and naturalization of gender identity theory in our everyday lives.

This is a delicate critique to offer insofar as meeting the conditions of the gender-affirming care model does provide some trans people (usually affluent, white trans people) a pathway to embodying who they are. Yet there is a difference between making a critique that diminishes the life chances of trans people and one that seeks to expand them. It is one thing to point out how the dominant model of affirmation perpetuates dominant notions of gender at the expense of more expansive possibilities for existence, and another to insist on banning access to care and transition because the notion of gender identity is complicated. Regardless, however, there is no doubt that gender-affirming care *does save lives*. But anti-trans efforts that work to erode the gender-affirming care model by insisting on the danger of care and the problems with the gender identity model obscure what is most significant about affirmation. It is a matter of whether we conceive of another way to be in relation – of another way to become. This is precisely Beauvoir's concern in *The Ethics of Ambiguity* and *The Second Sex*. Do we foreclose freedom for the other for the sake of the serious world? Do we continue to confer meaning onto the singularity of existence for the sake of maintaining relations of subordination? Do we insist on the world of being or do we pursue an open becoming?

On Self-Determination

The invalidation of self-defined gender is a constitutive phenomenon in trans people's lives. This experience usually coincides with another phenomenon: the imposition and enforcement of gender that accords to conventional perception or **assigned gender**. These social rituals are so routine that their most frequent manifestations, the mundane ones, go unnoticed by non-trans people. For those who do notice them, who do live them, who do experience our self-defined gender as dismissed or regularly rendered suspect, these rituals compromise who we can become. They also disclose an integral structure to the dominant practice of gender – namely, a tyranny of **third-person authority over gender,** which normalizes and naturalizes a nonconsensual conferral of gender by others. In other words, gender is assigned to you by others (the "third person" or a view beyond the self); it is others who tell you who you are. It is so common for our bonds with others to be formed through such a conferral that it usually goes unnoticed and is rarely considered something to be concerned about. That is, of course, until trans people begin to speak from another location, that of **trans first-person authority** (FPA). In contrast to third-person authority, trans FPA insists that it is the individual who decides who they are as a gendered person. Typically, the matter of FPA in general raises the following question: Does the avowal of the first person – namely, what they say they know about their experience – hold authority, or is a third person in a better position to know? Philosopher Talia Bettcher offers an insightful response to this question about trans FPA, as a specific kind of FPA. Bettcher acknowledges that first-person authority is undoubtedly complicated by the fact that "denial, self-deception, wishful thinking, and unconscious attitudes are common (and detectable) in society" (2009, p. 100). That such dispositions are common means that what an individual claims to know about themselves could be misguided, a view regularly held by those seeking to ban access to gender-affirming medical care, especially for minors. Bettcher argues that suspicions of trans FPA are framed as an issue of epistemic authority, or as a matter of "who knows best," when in fact trans FPA is a matter of *ethical* authority.

To understand trans FPA as an ethical phenomenon, one needs to understand the harm of third-person authority over trans people's existence. In the dominant schema, gender is heavily constituted by what others say you are with specific regard to genital status, which is taken to be the reality of who you actually are. The conferral is rooted in assumptions and expectations about genital status based on the perception of gender presentation. In other words, if others perceive you to be a woman based on how you look, then they will expect that you do not have a penis, and not having a penis is what *really* makes you a woman. This belief about the meaning of genitals is why, for instance, genital inspections that confirm a person is who they say they are are taken to be the logical outcome of anti-trans legislation that targets trans participation in sports. While, as I soon discuss, this third-person authority can deauthorize the genders of some non-trans people, its harm is particularly tangible with regard to what it does to trans people. People whose self-relation to gender does not exclusively align with the gender conferred by third-person authority are routinely met with a constellation of hostile forces, the most basic of which is a denial of who they say they are. This denial is premised on the epistemic problem with FPA – namely, that one is engaged in self-deception, wishful thinking, or faulty knowing, or what Beauvoir would call bad faith, on the basis that who a trans person says they are is not premised on "the truth," that is, on their genital status. Bettcher names this denial of trans FPA the Basic denial of authenticity (BDA), which, as discussed in the Introduction, is a most basic kind of transphobia.

Importantly, the denial of trans FPA is not entirely the fault of a commitment to biological essentialism, or the belief that biology dictates who we are. The routine practice of third-person authority is also a pedagogy of gender. Third-person authority is not recognizing something about who we are; it is doing something to who we become. It instructs us into a mode of being. On the one hand, such a pedagogy authorizes biological essentialism, and, on the other, makes the reality and practice of self-defined gender nonsensical. As a pedagogy of gender, third-person authority teaches us that gender is not something we give ourselves. Who you "really" are is decided for you by others, a decision which is rooted in a certain belief about what constitutes the truth of who we are. The only acceptable first-person authority over gender is one that accords with what others say about who you "really" are. In effect, then, this method of gender rests on the refusal of trans first-person authority.

But what – or really who – exactly is being disclosed when a trans person asserts, "This is who I am," in the face of the third-person authorization of gender? It certainly is the case that trans FPA can be read as a knowledge claim about one's self. While some people might tell me I am a woman, which they know on the basis of an assumed genital status, my avowal can be read as a claim that I know otherwise. On the other hand, as Bettcher argues, when I assert "This is who I am," I am not *only* making an epistemic claim, and perhaps not even first and foremost. I am making a claim about who I am as a condition of possibility for being in the world with others. Trans FPA is therefore also an ethical avowal. By refusing the socially mandated avowal of genital–gender status enforced by third-person authority, a trans person discloses something about their self that bears social and personal significance that affects and shapes their existence and relations with others.

When read as a disclosure of existential self-identity, trans FPA is not a response to the question "What am I?" but it is a matter of avowing *who* one is. As Bettcher argues, this existential claim necessarily requires a commitment to one's values and thus speaks to and is a condition for an authentic relation to oneself, others, and the world at large. To put it another way, the avowal is profoundly entangled with a person's significance and capacity for acting in the world. The denial of trans FPA is thus a refusal of who a person is, and that refusal undermines their self-relation and relation to others. Given the tyranny of third-person authority, and the consequences that come from disobedience to it, this disclosure is existentially risky. The impossibility of such an avowal does not necessarily prevent engagement with one another, full stop, but it does compromise being in authentic relation to others.

In contrast to mainstream conceptions of authenticity, which are all about an individual having some transparent knowledge of themself, of really knowing who they are, Beauvoir offers a different conception of authenticity. For her, authenticity is not about transparency. There is no inner truth to discover, only the ceaseless creation of meaning and values. For Beauvoir, an individual's pursuit of authenticity isn't just for themself. It is a particular mode of being in relation with others. In this sense, authenticity is and is not an individual activity; it is mine to do and therefore it is an autonomous activity, but I do not undertake it only for my sake. And, contrary to views that posit authenticity as a quest for happiness, Beauvoir's authenticity is a pursuit of moral freedom, a kind of being-with. It is not about satisfaction or gratification, but responsibility. Beauvoirian authenticity is, then, a particular way of relating to ourselves, others, and the world through which we realize freedom. In other words, authenticity is about an ethical mode of relating to ourselves and to others – about becoming, not being.

To be clear, it's certainly true that third-person authority over gender makes possible a certain mode of being in relation: one rooted in authorizing the lives of others, one anchored to the conferral of meaning onto others. The affirmation of trans existence changes this reality not just for trans people, but for everyone. Affirming trans people restructures every encounter. That is, the key difference between third-person authority and trans FPA is a relational difference, a matter of how we relate to others. Instead of telling people who they are, of assuming who they are, the affirmation of trans existence requires us to practice relationality differently. Instead of the authoritative gesture of "This is what you are," the trans affirmation insists we ask, "How would you like me to refer to you?"

An Ethics of Trans Affirmation

The world that third-person authority over gender creates and the one made possible by affirming trans FPA have different structures of sociality and meaning-making. Third-person authority over gender is a particular way of making sense of one another in which gender is legislated to each of us. In this structure of meaning-making, we are assigned without our consent a mode of existence that we are expected to assume and we are punished if we do not. For those of who refuse the assignment, that punishment can be severe, even violent. The refusal itself can be a condition for your non-existence. In other words, "I" come to make sense in the perceptual field through an assignment that others give to me. As an assignment, it is meaning that is made of me, for me, by others, which both institutes and smothers me, but an individual cannot make that smothering go away on their own. Even if a person eventually assumes their assigned gender such that they give the assignment back to themself, it nevertheless is a result of being told what they are and how they should exist. This structure of engendering is what Beauvoir describes in Volume II of *The Second Sex*. It is how the infant becomes a girl who becomes a woman. Third-person authority, then, works to fix a sense of self, of who someone else is, through assignment, which should be understood not as referring to the mere assignment of linguistic markers but rather as the everyday administration of a narrow, totalizing, one-directional sense of gender.

Trans FPA offers an alternative structure of meaning-making and sociality. Instead of giving priority to others to tell me what I am, trans FPA prioritizes the sense an individual has of who they are in the world. It is the difference between relations predicated on power-over and those rooted in self-determination. But, far from an individualistic, neoliberal sense of self-determination that undercuts the significance of our bonds to others and how the world constrains our possibilities from the start, a trans conception of **gender self-determination** is socially attuned through and through. It's not a matter of becoming whoever you want to be without recognition of the world as it is; it's a matter of becoming who you need to become in this world, of creating possibilities for becoming in this world. It's a way to have a self-relation – to be such that you can actually show up with others in this world. As Eric Stanley puts it, "Gender self-determination is a collective praxis against the brutal pragmatism of the present, the liquidation of the past, and the austerity of the future. That is to say, it indexes a horizon of possibility already here, which struggles to make freedom flourish" (2014, p. 89). So, while the structure of meaning-making in trans FPA is one that comes from the self, rather than from others, it is not an enterprise of an unbounded self. Trans FPA is a different way of making gendered sense and meaning *with* others. It relies on an openness in communication and meaning – namely, that others don't impose meaning on an individual – but it is nonetheless a relational practice insofar as it *requires others* to hold possibility open for them, rather than close it down.

Trans FPA and the commitment to gender self-determination are, then, social practices. The individual avowal requires the affirmation of others. As Beauvoir says in *The Ethics of Ambiguity*, "the individual is defined only by his relationship to the world and to other individuals" ([1947] 1976, p. 156). Although such an avowal is made by a self for the possibility of becoming of a self, it is made for others as well. The avowal is a condition for living and being *with* others. In the absence of affirmation of trans FPA, an individual who makes that avowal will run up against third-person authority over gender. So, at stake in trans FPA is not

An Ethics of Trans Affirmation

only an individual's ethical avowal of who they are, but also the structuring of social interactions and how we make meaning together. In spaces created by and for trans people, this structure of sociality has long been at work. Spade, in writing about his pursuit for top surgery and experience of medical gatekeeping along the way, offers a good reminder about who already practices an affirmative, rather than authoritative, form of relationality. "I've found that in trans contexts, a much broader conception of trans experience exists," Spade writes; "The trans people I've met have shockingly believed what I say about my gender ... The people I've met share with me what my counselors do not: a commitment to gender self-determination and respect for all expressions of gender" (2013, p. 325).

It is true that many non-trans people are, and feel, stunted by normative expectations of them as men or as women. They, too, do not experience self-determination of the kind Spade has in mind. What an individual chooses to do with their negative affect toward expectations and impositions – how an individual assumes or negotiates their situation, as Beauvoir might say – might be one way to understand the difference between trans and non-trans experience. Nonetheless, when the tyranny of third-person authority prevails, the possibility for another way of living together, another way of creating and holding space for becoming, is foreclosed for all of us. The affirmation of trans FPA is thus not just about trans people; it is of how we live together and what meaning and values we prioritize.

Detransition and the Need for Ambiguity

At the age of 12, Chloe Cole came out to her parents as a transgender boy. Her parents took her to see a gender specialist and she was later diagnosed with gender dysphoria and thereafter put on puberty blockers. At age 13, she had her first testosterone injection and, 2 years later, at the age of 15, she had top surgery. On July 27, 2023, at the age of 19, Cole walked into the US Congress and gave this chronological account of her transition at a hearing titled "The Dangers and Due Process Violations of 'Gender-Affirming Care' for Children." Cole was present not as an advocate for gender-affirming care, but as a critic. "Hi, I'm Chloe Cole and I am a detransitioner," she said at the outset. She continues, "Another way to put that would be: I used to believe I was born in the wrong body, and adults in my life whom I trusted affirmed my belief, causing me lifelong, irreversible harm" (House Judiciary GOP, 2023). This was not the first time Cole had given testimony as a detransitioner. She began speaking out against gender-affirming care for minors in May 2022, testifying in support of the state of Ohio's House Bill 454, which would have banned gender-affirming care for minors had it passed. She has also given testimony in the American states of Florida, Utah, Kansas, Wyoming, and Tennessee in support of legislation that would ban gender-affirming care for minors, and has spoken out against legislation in the state of California that would make it a sanctuary state for trans kids, a bill that passed in January 2023.

Six years after she came out as transgender, Cole regularly speaks about her experience of gender affirmation as damaging, violent, and regretful. She describes her transition as ushered quickly along by doctors and supported by her parents who didn't know any better. She now understands her experience as a common struggle with puberty in a misogynist world. As she told US legislators, "I was intimidated by male attention and when I told my parents I felt like a boy, in retrospect all I meant was that I hated puberty, that I wanted this newfound sexual attention to go away, that I looked up to my brothers a bit more than my sisters" (House Judiciary GOP, 2023). On her own account, her desire to transition was rooted in the reality of misogyny, not in repressed gender identity that needed affirmation. The result of her prior feelings about being a boy was, according to her, a gross misdiagnosis from medical professionals. Cole, and her parents especially, couldn't see it as a gross misdiagnosis because it was obscured by the discourse of gender-affirmation, which pushed Cole down a rapid path of medical transition, ultimately causing her, she claims, irreversible damage.

Abigail Shrier's *Irreversible Damage: The Transgender Craze Seducing Our Daughters* (2020) makes almost the exact same argument as Cole regarding the problem with gender-affirming care for minors. Shrier insists that most adolescent "girls" who claim to be boys because they hate being a girl as they were assigned are not really trans. Despite what these adolescents say or feel about themselves as trans, Shrier claims what they're experiencing is the typical and terrible tradition of an adolescence shaped by misogyny. The problem, Shrier insists, is that in a world where gender-affirming care is allegedly rampant and medical transitions are made visible on social media by trans people, young "girls" become victims of a "transgender craze." They are ushered to doctors who affirm first-person authority, which then starts, according to Shrier, unrelenting medical interventions that cause irreversible physical and psychological harm under the guise of gender affirmation. Shrier and gender-critical feminists champion this critique of gender-affirming care and turn to detransitioners such as Cole as clear evidence of its truthfulness.

The most common rebuttal to the amplification of detransitioners' experience is that detransition is uncommon and views like Cole's, which seek to erode access to gender-affirming care based on the idea that it causes irreversible harm, diverge from the recommendations of major medical associations. It's true that such views do diverge from established, evidence-based medical care. It's also true that detransitioning is not a common phenomenon. It could also be true that Cole's experience should not be merely dismissed. It could also be true that there are others who describe their post-transition as one of dissatisfaction or regret and decide to detransition. These are experiences that should not be neglected. But they should also not be taken as indicative of a problem with gender-affirming care or as evidence that affirming trans FPA is irreversibly damaging.

Indeed, there is another way to think about the reality of transition: transition and detransition cannot be abstracted from the sociohistorical context in which they occur. In a world where being trans subjects an individual to judgment, suspicion, hostility, marginalization, discrimination, violence, and poverty, where being trans is taken to be pathological, non-desirable, and unattractive according to mainstream standards, it's not surprising that having one's experience of gender affirmed medically is not necessarily a total fix. In fact, living as trans might just be terrible, not because being trans is terrible, but because being trans in *this world* is. Even if uncommon, detransition is an experience of and from this world; it can't be read outside of it. Chloe Cole's experience is not just an experience of medical care; it's an experience of gender, transition, and post-transition feelings in a world where gender and being trans are charged. It's not possible to experience gender, either as a non-trans or trans person absent from the world in which it is lived, even if we tell ourselves this is the case. Cole's post-transition experience is just as much a reflection of this world – a world that is

An Ethics of Trans Affirmation

steadfast in pushing us into the realm of being, coercing us into and praising us for assuming gendered becoming that turns out to be *the fixedness of being*.

The problem, however, is that gender identity discourse, as well as anti-trans views, make the reality of how the world shapes and constrains who we are and who we can become unintelligible. Although its intention may be good, gender identity discourse that underlies gender-affirming care abstracts the lived experience of gender from the world in which it is lived, and, in doing so, offers an empty promise. Its emphasis on affirming an individual's inner sense of who they are as *the condition* for affirmation is an abstraction. It does not demand that external social and political conditions in which a particular self lives also need to change for trans FPA to be affirmed, to be experientially affirmative.

With regard to the affirmation of trans experience, the suggestion is that we cannot overlook or downplay the total situation in which transness – and gender and sex in general – is lived. Although, certainly, transness has something to do with an inner sense of self, it is not just that. There is also an entire worldly situation at play in all experience, an atmosphere that inflects and envelops each of us. We might speak in terms of there being an inner truth to who we are, but, if we follow Beauvoir, our lives and our selves are mired in ambiguity, by which she means that we are both subject and object, both free and products of our situation. This ambiguity doesn't need to mean one's experience of gender is ambiguous. Rather, it means that how, why, and from where our experience of gender comes is always ambiguous, for everyone. We always live gender in a world that conditions, shapes, and constitutes our experience, just as much as who we are and what bodies we have condition, shape, and constitute the world.

Accepting such ambiguity is not to diminish trans FPA or to inflate the experience of detransition, or vice versa. Rather, it is to acknowledge that a conception of trans affirmation that affirms only the inner self, and focuses on affirming the body because of an inner sense of self, will always be limited. It will always be an abstraction of our experience as in and of the world. The point here is not that trans FPA should not be affirmed. It's also not that gender-affirming care should not be available and accessible to trans people. Rather, the point is that gender affirmation must also be a worldly, social practice if anything about the engendering of our lived experience is to change.

In *The Ethics of Ambiguity* ([1947] 1976), Beauvoir argues that we flee the concreteness of our situations in favor of living and thinking in abstraction. When we do so, Beauvoir says, we also flee the ambiguity of our existence, reducing human existence to mind or matter. We tend to, she claims, disavow our ambiguity because it is easier, more comforting, more straightforward than embracing the indeterminacy, opacity, and uncertainty of being human. For instance, we are our bodies and we're also not simply bodies, but the tendency, Beauvoir says, is to insist that we either are our bodies and therefore determined by them, or are not our bodies and therefore are free of them. What we need to do instead, is embrace ambiguity, and not try to resolve it. To assume our ambiguity is, for Beauvoir, necessary if we are to live an ethical relation to becoming. At the same time, a key dimension of Beauvoir's avowal of ambiguity is that our becoming is uncertain and indeterminate. We may take risks and make decisions that we come to regret, that do not have the outcomes we had hoped for. This is the risk of freedom. That fact that freedom, that becoming, entails the possibility of being let down, of regret, of being unhappy, of detransitioning does not

An Ethics of Trans Affirmation

mean we should not pursue freedom. It does not mean gender-affirming care should be abolished.

As Beauvoir makes clear in *The Second Sex*, a key problem with becoming a woman is that it creates a condition of being in relation with others that disavows ambiguity. Becoming a woman compromises an individual's ability to assume ambiguity not just with herself, but in relation to others. She becomes her body, a subject split by how she is committed to be an object for others. This perversion of her ambiguity, namely being reduced to her body, entails a further distortion of ambiguity – namely, that her objectification is taken to be natural. When this is considered a natural phenomenon, the reality that external forces do shape who we are is erased. Moreover, the child who is assigned 'girl' and expected to become a woman is committed – by others and, over time, by herself – to living a life in which she flees her ambiguity. She is taught her assignment is destiny. She comes to embrace it as destiny. In doing so, the girl embraces herself as being, not becoming, and she does so not merely on her own behalf, but because of the influence of others. This influence of others bears down on her own agency; it undermines her capacity for self-definition and gender self-determination.

In the face of such influence, trans FPA makes a different claim and thus opens up another mode of relationality. Trans FPA does not make demands about who others should be. It does not expect others to become a certain way. It does not coerce others into being. It doesn't demand answers. It doesn't require explanation. It accepts that you are who you say you are, not who I demand you to be. It accepts that you or I may become in ways other than what is expected. It accepts that someone may not care to claim a gender. It affirms trans FPA regardless of the justification for transness because doing so is a condition of a gendered relationality that refuses power over others. This affirmation of trans FPA is thus a matter of affirming self-determination so that an individual can actually engage in the world as they choose, even if their choosing is already constrained and conditioned by the world. This affirmation is a refusal of relationality that reduces each of us to the expectations others have of us. It is to refuse relationality that demands we own up to what others say we are. The affirmation of trans FPA is, then, a condition of relationality that does not turn becoming into being.

This trans ethic of affirming self-determination does not neglect the influence of the world. From a Beauvoirian perspective, this is key. For Beauvoir, the influence of others and the world never goes away. We are not unbounded and purely free, but always constrained by the concrete situation in which we live. This means, too, that experiences of gender, trans and non-trans, are always under the influence of the world, always in relation, always constrained. They are never pure experiences of the inner life of an individual. Gender self-determination is never, then, pure freedom. This does not, however, mean that we must refuse trans FPA. Rather, insofar as gender self-determination is a relational gesture in which the relation between self and others holds open possibilities and indeterminacy and accepts the uncertainty about why and how we become differently, we must embrace trans FPA. It is the difference between demanding and coercing others into being, or of remaining in being by preventing transition, and opening up space for becoming.

This trans ethic of affirmation is likely not going to satisfy someone like Chloe Cole, her anti-trans supporters, or gender-critical feminists. It's not likely to convince them that gender-affirming care, especially for minors, isn't damaging. Their starting point is already skewed, however. The harm of third-person author-

An Ethics of Trans Affirmation

ity over our lives is unintelligible to them because they reduce human existence to biology. Such views about human existence more generally, and about gender-affirming care in particular, do not create the condition for ethical relations with ourselves or with others. It's true that there may be the possibility that gender-affirming care doesn't cure someone's dysphoria, but that's not the fault of gender-affirming care. That's the result of living gender in a world where relationality is damaged. Rather than foreclose our becoming, our starting point must be relations that hold it open.

Pronoun-Go-Rounds

It was around 2009, in my mid-20s, that I began to regularly refer to myself as genderqueer. At the time, it was the language I had access to that better approximated my lived experience. Regardless of how I understood myself, I was certain that most people would read me exclusively as a woman, so I used this term with myself and people I trusted would get it, without question. The rest of the time, I chose not to disclose anything about my gender. I let third-person authority over my existence play out as it usually does. I wasn't ashamed or embarrassed, I was just convinced it wouldn't make sense. And I didn't really care to spend my energy trying to make sense to others. In other words, the act of disclosure, of revealing myself to others, didn't feel like it would create the world I needed. Who was I becoming through the disclosure? Who might I become through nondisclosure? At the same time, I'd already gotten so accustomed to the expectation that others would assign meaning to me regardless that, in the face of the history and social practice of assignment, nondisclosure, not gendering myself to and for others, felt freeing. Today, I often use different language. But today, as in the past, I don't always or mostly push for this linguistic disclosure.

A few years later, pronouns became a thing and the requests for disclosure became a more prominent feature in my life. Not that they weren't a thing before. Choosing, creating, and disclosing pronouns had long been a practice in trans contexts. Dominant spaces, however, just did what had always been done: assume and assign binary gender pronouns based on assumptions about the meaning of your appearance. In my own experience, I can't point to an exact moment that the trans practice of pronoun disclosure spilled over to dominant spaces, but it now seems to be *the* thing people do to try to be affirming. In trans and some queer contexts, it feels ordinary and almost insignificant to share pronouns. In dominant spaces, the act of disclosure often feels different. The difference has to do with the fact that it wasn't and still isn't something non-trans people are used to, which makes the practice feel clunky and puts the spotlight on trans people. It also often feels disingenuous, as if pronoun disclosures will change things for trans people or about our lives more generally.

Pronoun-go-rounds are not a bastion against trans antagonisms, or even always good for trans people. There's plenty of debate amongst trans people as to what good pronominal revelation does. Disclosure, as an act of visibility, can subject trans people to scrutiny, to suspicion, to invalidation, and even physical harm. It can also reify, rather than undermine, the view that gender is an essential truth of a subject waiting to be revealed through enunciation. It's also the case that some of us just don't know or want to decide on our pronouns. The experience of gender ambiguity, ambivalence, opacity, and undecidability can be made invisible through the act of pronoun disclosure. This reality isn't necessarily a fault of the pronoun-go-round practice. It's a limit of language. Pronouns aren't going to tell us the whole truth about any of us. Asking for, rather than assuming, pronouns is, however, a mundane way to shift how we relate, from third-person authority over gender to trans FPA. The act of disclosure cannot operate as obligatory, as a mandate. It is also important that people cultivate an understanding of pronouns as only approximating a sense of who we are. They are not a revelation of some essential truth. Indeed, we're not going to create an ethics of gender just by getting people's pronouns right, but we also shouldn't just assume we know how to refer to people either and continue to assign gender based on those assumptions. That's a habit we should give up. At the same time, a focus on pronouns obscures more significant material needs and desires of trans people related to healthcare, employment, and housing.

In this chapter, I've insisted that we need a different conception of affirmation, one not anchored to the medical model, but rooted in an existentialist ethic of relationality. I've concluded by turning to pronouns because they are often centered as a practice of affirmation and trans inclusion. They should not be the main focus. But pronoun-go-rounds should not be trivialized or rejected outright either. They are also an attempt to create relational practices that undermine third-person authority. We need not simply accept the attempt, but we should continue to create practices that restructure meaning-making, for how the meaning of who we are is made and who gets to control how it is made matter. It is about sacrificing past beliefs and habits, and instituting new ways of living, individually and with others. This is also the ethical and political charge Beauvoir leaves us with at the end of *The Second Sex*. "She has to shed her old skin and cut her own clothes," Beauvoir writes; "She will only be able to do this if there is a collective change" (2010, p. 761).

Conclusion:
Bad Faith and Feminism

On March 18, 2023, as part of her "Let Women Speak" tour, UK-based gender-critical feminist Kellie-Jay Keen-Minshull, also known as Posie Parker, made a stop in Melbourne, Australia, for a scheduled visit to the Parliament House. She was there to advocate for the rights of women. Let Women Speak is part of Keen-Minshull's organization, Standing for Women, "a global women's movement that creates space for women to center women" (Let Women Speak, 2023). By women, Keen-Minshull means "natal women." As stated on the movement's website:

> It is essential that this word is retained to mean 'adult human female' only. Without this word all of our rights and protections are lost. Our rights were never created for our 'gender' but our sex ... Our sex is female ... If our rights become dependent upon 'gender' then they are no longer women's rights, they are 'feminine' rights. (Let Women Speak, 2023)

As part of her effort to spread anti-trans, gender-critical ideology worldwide, Keen-Minshull launched Let Women Speak to make sure "adult human females"

Conclusion: Bad Faith and Feminism

are not erased. "2023 is the year of the TERF," the website boldly declares (2023).

At the time of her visit, Keen-Minshull was barely known in Australia. British anti-trans activism wasn't yet soaking up mainstream airtime down under. But her visit was not without controversy. Advocates of trans people and trans rights showed up to protest. The unsuccessful candidate of Australia's Liberal Party, Katherine Deves, known for backing efforts to prevent trans women from participation in women's sports, was present and encouraging of Keen-Minshull's visit. So were 30 white men from the Nationalist Socialist network, who, like the far-right white nationalist groups in the United States, including Proud Boys and Patriot Front, are invested in and supportive of anti-trans politics. The group of men marched on the street near the Parliament House performing the Nazi salute, while goose-stepping, as Nazi soldiers did during the Third Reich. They also carried a banner that read: "Destroy Paedo Freaks" (Hansford, 2023).

Keen-Minshull distanced Let Women Speak from Nazi affiliation. Just a few years earlier in October 2019, she took a similar position when appearing in an interview with prominent YouTuber and French-Canadian white nationalist Jean-François Gariépy. She used the interview to disseminate her brand of gender-critical ideology, captured at the time by her hashtag #AdultHumanFemale. The interview has all the familiar notes of gender-critical views and politics. In response to criticism for appearing on Gariépy's YouTube channel, Keen-Minshull claimed to not know anything about his political views prior to the interview. She also added, "White supremacy and the racism that fuels it has no place in a civilised society, I abhor those views and the people that hold them. . . . These days so many people are called Nazis and far right that the prophetic warning that we will no longer recognise the real ones is beginning to come true" (Parsons, 2019).

Keen-Minshull and her campaign are certainly not white nationalist simply because white nationalists support her views. But it is also important not to overlook that white nationalist politics galvanize around gender-critical efforts like those of Let Women Speak. What is going on when this happens, even when white nationalism is denounced? Why are gender-critical efforts to regulate the meaning of 'woman,' to limit who can be a woman, desirable to the far-right? In her book, *Me Not You: The Trouble with Mainstream Feminism* (2020), Alison Phipps points out how feminist efforts, in the name of creating space for recognition of their experiences and protecting their rights, can nonetheless legitimate oppressive state systems, even when they say they are working against them. By acting as gatekeepers of 'woman,' gender-critical positions regulate and secure a grammar to 'woman,' a grammar that is appealing to other legacies of domination. From a Beauvoirian perspective, this appeal is something to take responsibility for. As she details in *The Ethics of Ambiguity*, we are all responsible for who takes up our appeals and how they do so. Feminist appeals are no different; every feminist must take responsibility for who responds to our appeals.

While some may find it a stretch to use the word 'feminist' to describe gender-critical feminism, it is certainly true that anti-trans views have a history within feminist politics, particularly the kind that centers the experiences of the most privileged of women, the kind that becomes popularized and digested by the mainstream. Such feminism – exemplified by early suffrage movements that only advocated for white women's right to vote, feminist-led campaigns to legalize birth control that were also rooted in racist eugenics projects, and the

Conclusion: Bad Faith and Feminism

homophobia central to the late 1960s and early 1970s women's liberation movement – should be considered feminism not because it's good feminism, but because it highlights how feminism has conspired with, and can be complicit with even when it says it is not, legacies of domination that target the most vulnerable of women and gender minorities. This is a point women of color feminist scholars and activists around the world have long insisted on.

When feminism conspires and is complicit with domination, it is a feminism in bad faith. This kind of feminism neglects, intentionally or not, to consider the sociohistorical circumstances that give shape to reality and that ignore, willfully or not, social customs *as norms*. By 'feminism in bad faith', I also mean a kind of feminism that erodes the possibility for freedom for all. Drawing on Beauvoir's notion of bad faith, I conclude here with an account of the bad faith of gender-critical feminists to expose how it annihilates freedom, bonds between individuals, and allows oppressive ideological constructs to persist at the level of our personal and social existence.

Being in Bad Faith

For Beauvoir, **bad faith** refers to a wide range of existential attitudes, or a disposition or way of assuming one's existence in the world, that allow us to flee from freedom and, in turn, allow us to flee responsibility for ourselves, others, and the world as it is. This flight is, on Beauvoir's account, rooted in a disavowal of our ambiguity – namely, that we are both facticity and transcendence, a point discussed in chapter 2. As she makes clear in *The Ethics of Ambiguity*, when individuals disavow ambiguity, they distance themselves from and obscure the reality of the human condition. In effect, an individual lives their life through an illusion of reality. For this reason, bad faith is a matter of deceiving oneself about the conditions of existence. So, for instance, to take up the view that human existence is pure facticity as gender-critical feminists do, is to disown the truth of being human. Their insistence that biology determines who we are doesn't require any engagement with the concrete conditions of existence, with the possibilities that do and do not exist, with the ways we as individuals are responsible for how the world is, and with how we can live gender. Ultimately, defining human existence by our facticity only sets up a deceptive reality, a distorted understanding of what it is to be human. The deception and distortion at the heart of gender-critical feminism are, on Beauvoir's terms, moral faults.

Beauvoir does not think bad faith always amounts to an ethical problem, but it often does. As she shows across her work, being in bad faith generates and structures unethical social, material, and political conditions. It creates such a world because an illusory engagement with the truth of our existence, has destructive effects on the relationship between self and others. When we are in bad faith, we avoid the truth of our existence, of our situation, of the conditions of our relations with others – the consequence of which is impoverished and often unethical social, political, and material circumstances. For instance, to neglect to consider how our own willing, how our transcendent activity, plays a key role in how the world is, and to claim, instead, that our biology dictates what we are, is to fail to wrestle with and own that we are in fact responsible for how the world unfolds, for what possibilities are open to us and which ones are not. This neglect, this failure, is, for Beauvoir, a condition from which freedom is denied. She thinks we often pursue bad faith, rather than freedom, to appease the anxiety that comes from realizing that what happens

Conclusion: Bad Faith and Feminism

in the world is up to us, which is to say, that we are responsible, not in the individualistic sense, but as individuals always in relation to others, for how the world is and who we can each become.

To pursue freedom is, for Beauvoir, not a matter of doing whatever we want. Her focus is on what she calls moral freedom, the pursuit and realization of ethical bonds with others. In contrast to individualistic notions of freedom, often central to Western liberal democracies such as the United States, Beauvoir takes freedom to be a matter of how we are in relation to ourselves and to others. Genuine or authentic freedom is not, then, a matter of self-interest, of acting and choosing however one wants, of believing whatever one wants or what is convenient. Rather, for Beauvoir, we are morally free, authentically free, when we cultivate self–other relations that hold open a future of possibilities for all people. She understands the realization of moral freedom as the benchmark of an ethical existence.

In her view, moral freedom requires that I forgo my own self-interests, my own will, my own life projects, when they jeopardize or foreclose the future possibilities of others. Moral freedom, then, requires a relational and material awareness, an engagement with what my actions and beliefs do and do not make possible for myself and others, and an effortful pursuit of social, political, economic conditions that open up the future for everyone, even if it requires that I do not get what I want or expect, even if it requires giving up conventions that I have taken to be natural.

She does not, however, think it is easy to realize moral freedom. In her view, whether we live in bad faith has much to do with what the material and political conditions of our lives offer us. Ignorance, social privilege, material affluence, and even social and material deprivation, as well as realities of oppression and trauma, can lure us into bad faith. So too can the conflict between our self-interests and those of others. It is often the case, Beauvoir insists, that how the world is set up, and how our lives are structured by its arrangements, not only lure us into bad faith, but even preempt a self-awareness that one is in bad faith. We just come to accept things the way they are. We might accept a version of ourselves, of others, or of the world just to get by. Even more perniciously and selfishly, an individual or group of individuals might secure a world that works better for them at the expense of others because it is easier than creating just conditions; it is easier than sacrificing the privilege and power one is accustomed to. Ultimately, we often flee our freedom and act in bad faith not only because it is often the easier choice, but also because we are enticed by others and by the structures of our lives.

In *The Second Sex*, Beauvoir considers how patriarchal values lure all individuals, women included, into bad faith. Indeed, a central claim she makes throughout the book is that patriarchal values, meanings, and conventions codify modes of bad faith into gendered subjectivity, which, in effect, conditions and concretizes oppression at the levels of the personal, social, and political. Not only does patriarchal ideology instruct us to believe that differences between men and women are biological, its gender arrangements also, Beauvoir claims, teach us to disavow our ambiguity. Beauvoir's account underscores how women are enticed into bad faith, but she is just as adamant that men are too. Indeed, on her account, the ideal of masculinity, and how that ideal is assumed or lived, encourages and demands that men disavow facticity, and all that is associated with it, including women. Ultimately, as philosopher Debra Bergoffen (2000) puts it, patriarchal ideology is a perversion of everyone's existence; it erodes our capacity for living in good faith with one another.

Conclusion: Bad Faith and Feminism

As chapter 1 discusses, the self-mutilation central to "becoming a woman" denies the person instructed and coerced into womanhood her transcendence. This self-mutilation is what draws a woman into bad faith. In a patriarchal situation, women are, Beauvoir argues, ruptured from their transcendence, and anchored in the realm of facticity, including being reduced to their bodies and to an objectifying passivity, which, on her account, sets women up to be, and often to accept being, sexualized prey. Although Beauvoir does not believe women are mere victims in such a set-up, she does believe they are enticed by the modicum of recognition they receive if they take up their own self-mutilation. This recognition is powerful; paradoxically, it gives women a limited access to freedom. By behaving according to the rules of patriarchy, they get propped up, their voices might even be heard, perhaps they are even offered a platform. Such complicity is a trap, of course. It's not a condition of moral freedom, but the praise and recognition received as a result of confirming patriarchal ideology is real and tangible. Insofar as moral freedom requires relations in which all are free, under patriarchal conditions of relationality, under patriarchal gender, moral freedom is compromised.

It's significant that Beauvoir's account of bad faith in *The Second Sex* has everything to do with a sociohistorical norm of becoming a woman. Those who become women in the way Beauvoir describes, those who are instructed to become women in the way she describes, have historically been white, middle- and upper-class, non-trans girls and women. As a result, such women are likely to be bad-faith actors because they have been socialized to be. This is neither to say that others cannot and do not act in bad faith as a result of assuming patriarchal ideology and gender, nor to say that all such women who are bad-faith actors are doomed to be, or are, people we should feel sorry for when they are. Rather, the point here is that when such individuals do live in bad faith, it is a result of maintaining conditions that secure for themselves a sliver of recognition. The moral fault is that it does so at the expense of the freedom of others.

Feminism in Bad Faith

Gender-critical feminism, trans-exclusionary radical feminism, are in bad faith. They are feminisms that disavow ambiguity and foreclose relational and material conditions necessary to moral freedom. Their disavowal is rooted in taking a key dimension of social life, one constitutive of how we are in the world – that is, the phenomenon of being a man or a woman – as pure facticity. From this view, they justify the oppression of trans people. From this view, they advocate and bolster material conditions that not only foreclose trans people's futures, but also entrench gender ideology rooted in annihilating the possibility of moral freedom.

Such feminisms claim to advocate for women. They claim to be about protecting women. They do in fact advocate for *some* women. They do in fact protect *some* women. But they do not pursue conditions of existence that open possibilities for all. They pursue conditions of existence that open possibilities for some, at the expense of others. Beauvoir's feminism, a feminism of freedom, does not condone such political action. Beauvoir's feminism supports political efforts that work to secure freedom, relationally or materially, for all.

Beauvoir's feminist commitments make moral demands on how we live together. As should now be clear, her view is not that we are biologically destined to be men or women. We do, then, have a choice to make about how we assume, individually and col-

Conclusion: Bad Faith and Feminism

lectively, our becoming. Such a choice is not without constraint. Historical legacies, social norms of gender, ideological beliefs about bodies, and the reality of our facticity are all constraints we must struggle with, come to terms with. Doing so is not easy; we aren't transparent to ourselves. Our existence, our desires, our goals, our complicity with norms and with realities of oppression are not always obvious. We cannot overcome our bodies, but we can modify and alter them. Even in the face of constraint, of a bounded freedom, Beauvoir nevertheless insists that we can and ought to pursue political action for the sake of moral freedom, for the sake of creating relations with ourselves and others that open possibility. For her, that action cannot be simply performative; we can't just say we support freedom for all; we must pursue, through our individual actions, material change. Beauvoir's existentialist ethics might not contain the answer for what institutions with state power need to do. Her ethics are, however, instructive with regard to how we ought to live. We can refuse to accept and justify the conditions of a world in which the annihilation of trans existence is possible. We can choose to affirm who people say they are. We can choose to affirm trans desires. We can choose to create a world wherein becoming is an open field of possibilities, where trans existence is materially possible.

Glossary

Ambiguity Beauvoir's conception that to be human is to always be both subject and object, mind and matter, transcendence and facticity, free and constrained. For Beauvoir, although humans try to flee our ambiguity, reducing ourselves to either mind or matter, to either being pure freedom or purely determined, we should embrace our ambiguity.

Assigned gender The imposition and enforcement of gender by others that accords with conventional perception and social and historical norms.

Bad faith A wide range of existential attitudes, or a disposition or way of assuming one's existence in the world, that allow us to flee from freedom and, in turn, allow us to flee responsibility for ourselves, others, and the world.

Basic denial of authenticity (BDA) Coined by philosopher Talia Bettcher, this is a basic kind of transphobia, understood as the denial of who trans people say they are. BDA relies on a way of knowing that insists that the truth of a person's gender is to be determined by genitalia, and the expectation is that this truth can be

Glossary

read or known by others through an individual's gender presentation.

Becoming Refers to the reality of a thing or of existence as indeterminate, historically bound, and contingent.

Being A philosophical concept that refers to an internal, predetermined, and unchanging essence of a thing.

Biological essentialism The belief that physiology or biology fully determines who one is. In relation to gender, this belief means that 'woman' is a biological phenomenon, meaning that who is a woman is determined by biology.

Facticity The factical dimension of our lives, the ones that are inevitable, such as the reality that there are others in the world or that humans, as a species, have basic needs that must be met to stay alive.

Gatekeeping Efforts to control and limit access to transition-related care and services, especially by those in positions of power.

Gender-affirming care A wide range of social, psychological, and medical interventions that support an individual's gender identity when it is incongruent with their gender or sex designated at birth.

Gender-critical feminism/feminists A feminist movement and individual feminists who espouse biological essentialism, claiming that biology is what makes one a real woman or man, which inevitably invalidates trans existence. The gender-critical view advocates only for natal women.

Glossary

Gender identity theory A psychological theory that distinguishes between biological sex and gender and proses that gender identity is an internal, psychological phenomenon.

Gender self-determination A collective practice of gender freedom that prioritizes trans FPA and the practice of self-defined gender, and thus challenges the tyranny of third-person authority over gender.

Immanence The term Beauvoir uses in *The Second Sex* to describe the passive and cyclical aspects of being human, which she understands to be related to the factical dimension of human existence.

Moral freedom A conception of freedom that Beauvoir understands as a kind of social bond or mode of relationality in which we strive to live in ways that hold open possibilities for one another.

Natal woman A concept used by gender-critical feminists that defines 'woman' as a biologically determined category. A natal woman is a woman by virtue of her biology.

Natural attitude Our everyday, ordinary perception, or what we take for granted. It is that which we see and experience as a matter of fact, as "just the way things are." For a phenomenologist like Beauvoir, it is necessary to expose and engage the natural attitude, to critique it, and not to accept it as fact.

Phenomenology A philosophical method and tradition that studies "things" or phenomena of the world from the perspective of first-person, embodied experience – i.e., "things" as they are lived.

Glossary

Relative existence A concept Beauvoir uses in *The Second Sex* to name what it is to become a woman in a patriarchal world. For her, to become a woman is to assume an existence that is defined through and always in relation to – which is to say relative to – men.

Self-defined gender In contrast to assigned gender, adopting self-defined gender is the practice by which an individual decides who they are as a gendered person.

Sex–gender distinction Originally thematized by psychologists John Money and Robert Stoller in the 1950s and appropriated by feminists in the 1970s, this distinction claims sex is a biological phenomenon, while gender is a social, cultural, and psychological one.

Situation The total, concrete condition of individual existence. For Beauvoir, an individual's situation includes bodily, social, historical, economic, and political dimensions.

Social destiny In contrast to biological essentialism that claims our fate is dictated and decided for us by our biology, a social destiny refers to how the circumstances of the world in which one lives, including how others impact personal experience, can be so heavy-handed that they lay out a fate that is quasi-determinative. Beauvoir takes "becoming a woman" to be a social destiny.

Third-person authority over gender The dominant, Western practice of gender whereby not only do others decide what your gender is, but their decision is what matters; it has authority. This social custom normalizes and naturalizes a nonconsensual conferral of gender by others.

Glossary

Trans/Transgender As used in this book, these terms refer to people who move away from an assigned gender, an unchosen starting place, to a self-defined gender, regardless of how or whether a person undergoes any kind of social or medical transition. The term need not designate an identity.

Trans antagonisms The constellation of hostile forces, including gender-critical ideology and anti-trans legislation, that undermine trans life here and now and the possibility for trans existence in the future.

Trans-exclusionary radical feminist (TERF) Names a person, usually a non-trans woman, who claims to be a feminist, who supports the freedom of women and stands against the injustice of patriarchal domination, but also espouses views or offers support for views that, in various ways, delegitimize the existence of transgender people. TERFs have been vocal in Western feminist movements since at least the 1970s.

Trans first-person authority (FPA) A trans social practice through which an individual decides who they are as a gendered person and their self-definition holds authority.

Transcendence Beauvoir uses this term to refer to the meaning-making and world-building dimension of our lives. She understands it as future-oriented and related to the movement of freedom.

Transphobia Commonly understood as negative, prejudicial, hostile, or violent attitudes or actions toward transgender people. Such a conception of transphobia tends to overly individualize and pathologize its reality, framing transphobia as enacted only by a few "bad apples" rather than as a normalized and systemic reality, one woven into the social fabric, in which trans people are viewed as suspicious, deceivers, pretenders, and subjected to scrutiny and surveillance for being who they are.

Transsexual This concept typically refers to a person whose gender does not align with an assignment of and expectations around sexed embodiment and who has undergone medical reassignment to alter their bodies. While it is often claimed to be a pejorative term, some people do self-define as transsexual.

References

Awkward-Rich, Cameron (2022) *The Terrible We: Thinking with Trans Maladjustment*. Durham: Duke University Press.

Beauvoir, Simone de ([1947] 1976) *The Ethics of Ambiguity*. Trans. Bernard Frechtman. New York: Citadel Press.

Beauvoir, Simone de (1949a) *Le Deuxième Sexe I*. Paris: Gallimard.

Beauvoir, Simone de (1949b) *Le Deuxième Sexe II*. Paris: Gallimard.

Beauvoir, Simone de (2010) *The Second Sex*. Trans. Constance Borde and Sheila Malovany-Chevallier. New York: Alfred Knopf.

Bergoffen, Debra (2000) "From Husserl to Beauvoir: Gendering the Perceiving Subject." In Linda Fisher and Lester Embree (eds.) *Feminist Phenomenology*. Dordrecht: Kluwer Academic Publishers, pp. 50–70.

Bergoffen, Debra (2017) "The Floating 'a.'" In Bonnie Mann and Martina Ferrari (eds.) *"On ne naît pas femme: on le devient": The Life of a Sentence*. Oxford University Press, pp. 143–58.

Bettcher, Talia Mae (2006) "Appearance, Reality, and Gender Deception: Reflections on Trans-phobic Violence and the

References

Politics of Pretence." In Felix Ó Murchadha (ed.) *Violence, Victims, and Justifications: Philosophical Approaches*. New York: Peter Lang, 2006, pp. 174–200.

Bettcher, Talia Mae (2009) "Trans Identities and First-Person Authority." In Laurie Shrage (ed.) *You've Changed: Sex Reassignment and Personal Identity*. Oxford University Press, pp. 98–120.

Bindel, Julie (2021) "Janice Raymond: The Original Terf." Unherd, November 26. Available at: https://unherd.com/2021/11/meet-the-original-terf.

Braidwood, Ella (2018) "University Lecturer Criticised after Declaring 'Trans Women Are Still Males with Male Genitalia.'" Pink News, July 6. Available at: www.thepinknews.com/2018/07/06/university-lecturer-says-trans-women-are-still-males-with-male-genitalia.

Bretín, Rut de las Heras (2021) "Cuestión de educación: hace unos días, la fachada de la librería Mary Read fue vandalizada con unas pintadas tránsfobas." *El País*, August 23. Available at: https://elpais.com/espana/madrid/2021-08-24/cuestion-de-educacion.html.

Burke, Megan (2017) "Becoming A Woman: Beauvoir's Response to the Woman Question." In Bonnie Mann and Martina Ferrari (eds.) *"On ne naît pas femme: on le devient": The Life of a Sentence*. Oxford University Press, pp. 159–74.

Chu, Andrea Long (2018) "My New Vagina Won't Make Me Happy." *New York Times*, November 24. Available at: www.nytimes.com/2018/11/24/opinion/sunday/vaginoplasty-transgender-medicine.html.

Chu, Andrea Long (2024) "Freedom of Sex: The Moral Case for Letting Trans Kids Change Their Bodies." *New York Magazine*, March 11. Available at: https://nymag.com/intelligencer/article/trans-rights-biological-sex-gender-judith-butler.html.

Currah, Paisley (2022) *Sex Is as Sex Does: Governing Transgender Identity*. New York University Press.

References

Davis, Angela (1981) *Women, Race, & Class.* New York: Random House, 1981.

Duster, Chandelis (2021) "Marjorie Taylor Greene Posts Anti-transgender Sign across Hall from Lawmaker with Transgender Child." CNN, February 25. Available at: www.cnn.com/2021/02/25/politics/marjorie-taylor-greene-anti-transgender-sign/index.html.

Feinberg, Leslie (2014) *Stone Butch Blues.* 20th Anniversary Author Edition. Available at: https://leslie feinberg.net/wp-content/uploads/2015/08/Stone-Butch-Blues-by-Leslie-Feinberg.pdf.

Gill-Peterson, Jules (2018) *Histories of the Transgender Child.* Minneapolis: University of Minnesota Press.

Gluck, Genevieve (2021) "Interview: Dr. Kathleen Stock on Why We Need to Discuss Gender Identity in Philosophy." July 9. Available at: www.feministcurrent.com/2021/07/09/interview-dr-kathleen-stock-on-why-we-need-to-dis cuss-gender-identity-in-philosophy.

Hansford, Amelia (2023) "Trans Rights Protester Met with Nazis at Posie Parker Rally Recounts 'Terrifying Chaos.'" Pink News, March 24. Available at: www.thepinknews .com/2023/03/24/lilah-lilahrpg-posie-parker-kellie-jay-keen-minshull.

Hartman, Saidiya (1997) *Scenes of Subjection.* Oxford University Press.

Heinämaa, Sara (2003) *Toward a Phenomenology of Sexual Difference: Husserl, Merleau-Ponty, and Beauvoir.* Lanham: Rowman & Littlefield.

House Judiciary GOP (2023) "The Dangers and Due Process Violations of 'Gender-Affirming Care' for Children." Available at: www.youtube.com/watch?v=ts0ESOMKUKU.

Jeffreys, Sheila (2014) *Gender Hurts: A Feminist Analysis of the Politics of Transgenderism.* New York and London: Routledge.

References

Killermann, Sam (2018) "The Genderbread Person v4." Available at: www.itspronouncedmetrosexual.com/2018/10/the-genderbread-person-v4.

Lavery, Grace (2023) "Gender Criticism versus Gender Abolition: On Three Recent Books about Gender." *Los Angeles Review of Books*, July 31. Available at: https://lareviewofbooks.org/article/gender-criticism-versus-gender-abolition-on-three-recent-books-about-gender.

Lawford-Smith, Holly (2022) *Gender-Critical Feminism*. Oxford University Press.

Lawford-Smith, Holly (2023) *Sex Matters: Essays in Gender-Critical Philosophy*. Oxford University Press.

Let Women Speak (2023) Available at: www.standingforwomen.com.

Loffman, Matt (2021) "New Poll Shows Americans Overwhelmingly Oppose Anti-transgender Laws." PBS, April 16. Available at: www.pbs.org/newshour/politics/new-poll-shows-americans-overwhelmingly-oppose-anti-transgender-laws.

Lorber, Judith (1994) *Paradoxes of Gender*. New Haven and London: Yale University Press.

Lugones, María (2007). "Heterosexualism and the Colonial/Modern Gender System." *Hypatia*, 22(1): 186–209.

Mann, Bonnie (2017) "Beauvoir against Objectivism: The Operation of the Norm in Beauvoir and Butler." In Bonnie Mann and Martina Ferrari (eds.) *"On ne naît pas femme: on le devient": The Life of a Sentence*. Oxford University Press, pp. 37–54.

Marvin, Amy (2020) "Transsexuality, the Curio, and the Transgender Tipping Point." In Perry Zurn and Arjun Shankar (eds.) *Curiosity Studies: A New Ecology of Knowledge*. Minneapolis: University of Minnesota Press, pp. 188–208.

McArdle, Maëlys (2021) "Trans Rights Posters Vandalized." Maëlys blog, April 7. Available at: www.maelys.bio/2021/04/trans-rights-posters-vandalized.

References

McWeeny, Jennifer (2023) "Sex in *The Second Sex*: Beauvoir's Phenomenological Concept of 'Female.'" Paper presented at the Hypatia 40th Anniversary Conference, Eugene, Oregon, September 9.

Moi, Toril (2001) *What Is a Woman? And Other Essays*. Oxford University Press.

Parsons, Vic (2019) "Gender-Critical Feminist Posie Parker in Video with White Nationalist YouTuber – and a Lot of Mumsnet Users Are Fine with It." Pink News, October 15. Available at: www.thepinknews.com/2019/10/15/gender-critical-posie-parker-interview-jean-francois-gariepy-mumsnet.

Pew Research Center (2022) "Views of Laws and Policies Related to Transgender Issues Differ Widely by Party." June 23. Available at: www.pewresearch.org/social-trends/2022/06/28/americans-complex-views-on-gender-identity-and-transgender-issues/psdt_06-28-22_gender_identity_0_2.

Phipps, Alison (2020) *Me Not You: The Trouble with Mainstream Feminism*. Manchester University Press.

Raymond, Janice (1979) *The Transsexual Empire: The Making of the She-Male*. Boston: Beacon Press.

Raymond, Janice (1994) *The Transsexual Empire: The Making of the She-Male*. Reissue Edition. New York and London: Teachers College Press.

Rowling, J. K. (2020a) "J. K. Rowling Writes about Her Reasons for Speaking Out on Sex and Gender Issues." June 10. Available at: www.jkrowling.com/opinions/j-k-rowling-writes-about-her-reasons-for-speaking-out-on-sex-and-gender-issues.

Rowling, J. K. (2020b) [X] @jk_rowling. "'People Who Menstruate.'" June 6. Available at: https://x.com/jk_rowling/status/1269382518362509313?s=20.

Rowling, J. K. (2020c) [X] @jk_rowling. "If Sex Isn't Real." June 6. Available at: https://x.com/jk_rowling/status/1269389298664701952?s=20.

References

Santhanam, Laura (2023) "Majority of Americans Reject Anti-trans Bills, but Support for This Restriction is Rising." PBS, March 29. Available at: www.pbs.org/newshour/politics/majority-of-americans-reject-anti-trans-bills-but-support-for-this-restriction-is-rising.

Shrier, Abigail (2020) *Irreversible Damage: The Transgender Craze Seducing Our Daughters*. Washington, DC: Regnery Publishing.

Snorton, C. Riley (2017) *Black on Both Sides: A Racial History of Trans Identity*. Minneapolis: University of Minnesota Press.

Sommer, Marni, Kamowa, V., and Mahon, T. (2020) "Creating a More Equal Post-COVID-19 World for People Who Menstruate." Devex, May 28. Available at: www.devex.com/news/sponsored/opinion-creating-a-more-equal-post-covid-19-world-for-people-who-menstruate-97312#.XtwLnv0aEeR.twitter.

Spade, Dean (2011) *Normal Life: Administrative Violence, Critical Trans Politics, & the Limits of the Law*. Cambridge: South End Press.

Spade, Dean (2013) "Mutilating Gender." In Susan Stryker and Aren Aizura (eds.) *The Transgender Studies Reader*, 1st edition. New York: Routledge, pp. 315–32.

Stanley, Eric A. (2014) "Gender Self-Determination." *Transgender Studies Quarterly* 1(1–2): 89–91.

Stock, Kathleen (2021) *Material Girls: Why Reality Matters for Feminism*. London: Fleet.

Stryker, Susan (2008) *Transgender History*. Berkeley: Seal Press.

WPATH (World Professional Association for Transgender Health) (2011) *Standards of Care for the Health of Transsexual, Transgender, and Gender Nonconforming People*, 7th edition. Available at: www.wpath.org/media/cms/Documents/SOC%20v7/Standards%20of%20Care%20V7%20-%202011%20WPATH.pdf.

References

WPATH (World Professional Association for Transgender Health) (2023) "Statement of Opposition to Legislation Banning Access to Gender-Affirming Health Care in the US," March 8. Available at: www.wpath.org/media/cms/Documents/Public%20Policies/2023/USPATH_WPATH%20Statement%20re_%20GAHC%20march%208%202023.pdf.

Zurn, Perry (2021) *Curiosity and Power*. Minneapolis: University of Minnesota Press.